RETURN
to the
MYSTERY SCHOOL

Regaining the Edenic Consciousness

MAITREYA MYSTERY SCHOOL SERIES

RETURN to the MYSTERY SCHOOL

Regaining the Edenic Consciousness

ELIZABETH CLARE PROPHET

SUMMIT UNIVERSITY PRESS®

Gardiner, Montana

RETURN TO THE MYSTERY SCHOOL
Regaining the Edenic Consciousness
by Elizabeth Clare Prophet
Copyright © 2024 The Summit Lighthouse, Inc. All rights reserved.

Except for a single copy for your personal, noncommercial use, no part of this work may be used, reproduced, stored, posted or transmitted in any manner or medium whatsoever without written permission, except by a reviewer who may quote brief passages in a review.

For information, contact
The Summit Lighthouse, 63 Summit Way, Gardiner, MT 59030 USA
Tel: 1-800-245-5445 or 1 406-848-9500
info@SummitUniversityPress.com
www.SummitLighthouse.org

Library of Congress Control Number: 2024946966
ISBN: 978-1-60988-500-7 (softbound)
ISBN: 978-1-60988-501-4 (eBook)

SUMMIT UNIVERSITY 🔥 PRESS®

The Summit Lighthouse, Summit University, Summit University Press, 🔥, Church Universal and Triumphant, Keepers of the Flame, and *Pearls of Wisdom* are trademarks registered in the U.S. Patent and Trademark Office and in other countries. All rights reserved.

27 26 25 24   1 2 3 4

CONTENTS

From the Coming Buddha Who Has Come vii

INTRODUCTION ix
Return to the Mystery School

CHAPTER 1 . . . . (October 10, 1975)   1
Initiation for the New Day

CHAPTER 2 . . . . (October 19, 1975) 13
The Exchange of the Cosmic Cubes

CHAPTER 3 . . . . (December 31, 1975) 19
Expect the Unexpected

CHAPTER 4 . . . . (December 3, 1977) 31
The Wooden Begging Bowl

CHAPTER 5 . . . . (July 2, 1978) 39
Find Your Way Back to Me

CHAPTER 6 . . . . (December 31, 1978) 65
The Initiation of the Law of the One
in the Guru-Chela Relationship

CHAPTER 7 . . . . (February 4, 1979) 85
The Garden of Eden
    Removing the Splinters from the Soul

The Chart of Your Divine Self 104

Decrees & the Science of the Spoken Word 110

The Sacred Gift of the Violet Flame 117

CHAPTER 8 . . . . (March 24, 1979) 122
The Oscillation of Light for the Alignment of Your Soul

CHAPTER 9 . . . . (December 29, 1979) 136
A Meditation on the Glorious Mission of Our Brotherhood

CHAPTER 10 . . . . (December 4, 1980) 146
Love of the Person and the Law of the Word: God and My Right
The Ritual of the Great Interchange

CHAPTER 11 . . . . (April 19, 1981) 166
The Dilemma of the Soul in the Evolutionary Cosmos

CHAPTER 12 . . . . (July 1, 1981) 178
The Visitation of the Stars

CHAPTER 13 . . . . (July 19, 1981) 188
The Dispensation of the Righteous Branch

CHAPTER 14 . . . . (April 4, 1982) 196
The Living Book

CHAPTER 15 . . . . (January 2, 1983) 208
In the Heart of the One Sent

NOTES 217

From the Coming Buddha Who Has Come

I AM Buddha, I AM Mother. I stand betwixt time and space, the master of both. Yet I abide in neither, but I abide in the heart of the chela and in the stupa* of the Buddha. I come out of the Tushita heaven,† where I have been discoursing this night with bodhisattvas who have attained to that level of God Self-mastery and enlightenment. When you attain to that level, beloved, you may also go there; for this is a plane of heaven that is reserved for those having this or a greater attainment.

Thus, in many art forms you will see depicted the Buddha surrounded by many bodhisattvas in this heaven. These blessed unascended ones look to the day of my coming in the earth when they may reincarnate with me to be messengers of the Dharma of the New Age. They are filled with wonder that intimations of this Dharma and full cups of it are given through the dictations of the ascended masters through the messengers, that those in embodiment who are also on the path of the bodhisattva may be forerunners and indeed anchor the New Age of Aquarius for our coming.

I am here, beloved, in the fullness of the Coming Buddha who has indeed come. But I may one day come with my bodhisattvas to a certain level of incarnation if there shall be a golden age

---
**Stupa:* a domed structure serving as a Buddhist shrine
†*Tushita heaven:* the level of the etheric octave, or the plane of heaven, that is reserved for those having bodhisattva attainment or greater

upon earth. Thus many sweet smiling faces of these blessed ones look upon you as their point of hope for fulfillment of the long-awaited dream. It is their dharma to embody whether or not I do; for they must fulfill their path of the ascension and, in the process, become teachers of the Dharma.*

---

*Lord Maitreya, January 7, 1990

INTRODUCTION

Return to the Mystery School

Lord Maitreya, well known to Buddhists the world around as the Cosmic Buddha, has come to initiate those who would be his students. He bids you to answer his call: "Come Home to the heart of Maitreya."

And so he pondered and prayed for guidance on how to draw his disciples back to his heart:

> One day I sat, my head in my hand, deep in thought, and Lord Gautama said to me, "What are you thinking, my son?" And I said, "My father, can we win them with kindness and with love? Will they respond to love?" And my father said to me, "If you hold within your heart, my son, the full orchestration of love, 144,000 tones of love; if you yourself will come to know love, then yes, you will win them with love."
>
> My heart leaped for joy. My father had given to me the challenge to know love, to be love, not for the sake of mere love and loving love, not for the mere sake of the bliss of the communion of love, but for the salvation of souls, for the reaching out unto my God in humanity.*

---

*Lord Maitreya, November 21, 1976

After pondering this profound understanding, he later spoke to souls of his own—souls of the lineage of Sanat Kumara who are meant to outpicture Maitreya's path of love in all of its wondrous aspects in the New Age:

> One tender smile is surely worth a thousand frames of the face of Maitreya. The loving, overflowing, pure heart's giving—does this not convey the Maitreya beyond the veil?
>
> I desire you to be myself, not in pomposity or pride (now self-styled initiators of lesser mortals), nay, but to remember that by the grace of the one who has sent me, you yourself might be my vessel. . . .
>
> You shall surely know the Buddha in the Way when you expand the golden pink glow-ray of the heart, becoming thereby tender, sensitive, loving in a beautiful sound of love—love as appreciation for the soul, for the spirit, for the vastness of potential and being, but above all, appreciation for the God flame.*

Through the mists of time—from thousands of years ago in eras of unrecorded history, from the mystery schools now submerged on the continent of Lemuria that once thrived off the coast of California, the mystery schools of the ancient world of India, Greece, South America, Britain, and more recently in the United States—we hear echoed in our heart and soul Lord Maitreya beckoning us to the highest expression of our individual oneness with God.

Lord Maitreya has been with us when we couldn't hear him, so caught up we've been in our many lifetimes of karmic weavings through the centuries. Did he leave us, or did we leave him?

---

*Lord Maitreya, June 30, 1988

The light is always present, but the darkness of our wanderings has left us adrift. No more! Maitreya is calling us Home.

In the not-too-distant past, Maitreya came to give us his Word that would appease the pain of separation—our own and his. He has spoken in recent times when the one prepared to receive his Word and convey his testings, his path of initiation to us, was among us. This was his disciple of many incarnations, Elizabeth Clare Prophet, who received many dissertations from Lord Maitreya—all meant for those who hear his inner calling of the heart and have now found him through his words presented in this book. His words are cups of light for us to absorb and then prove his teachings by manifesting those 144,000 archetypal tones of love in action.

Maitreya's Mystery School was and is. It was here in Montana that Elizabeth Clare Prophet, who was anointed as the messenger of the ascended masters East and West, received the words of wisdom of Lord Maitreya and brought forth the teachings of the mystery school to those who experienced, and experience today, the testings of the path of initiation in the Aquarian age—the platform in time and space on earth for Maitreya to reveal his return through his own.

Maitreya's Mystery School is a personal experience. It is the testing of the soul in an exact manner that calls the soul to overcome the karma, the blind spots, the need for inner reckoning, all of which lead to the soul's victory, called the ascension.

The tremendous teachings that you will find within these fifteen chapters were delivered through the messenger Elizabeth Clare Prophet in the 1970s and 1980s. Just as the prophets in the Old Testament, her soul's surrender to God and her acceptance of her Higher Self, her Inner Christ, over the centuries, allowed Lord Maitreya and others of the ascended masters to deliver their Word.

Maitreya's Mystery School remained in this personal form until the retirement of the messenger from active, outer service in 1999 and her subsequent passing and ascension in 2009. After this period, the Mystery School took on a different form. Since Maitreya was no longer with his students personally through the person of the messenger, there were no longer live dissertations, and direct initiations would no longer be given. However, the full collection of Maitreya's teachings remain with us to study and assimilate as Maitreya initiates his students and disciples from the inner planes of light—the heavenly realms where we may commune with Lord Maitreya and attend the universities of the Spirit in our finer bodies as we sleep.

Thus there has been and there is today the return to Maitreya's Mystery School. Read his Word. Hear his Call. Walk the Path. And find your way Home to Lord Maitreya, whose name means *kindness*.

*This is the meaning
of the path of initiation—
that increment by increment,
line by line,
the acceleration of consciousness,
of light and light's determination,
takes place within you.*

CHAPTER 1

Initiation for the New Day

Initiation for the New Day is initiation for the new consciousness, which when it is put on as the garment of God, so far transcends the former state as to make that new consciousness incomprehensible to your present awareness, and that present awareness incomprehensible to the new consciousness. The leap, the arc of transition, is from the not-self to the Real Self—from that which was dead to the light, to that which is quickened in the flame.

How can we explain? How can we tutor the mind and heart at this level of awareness in that which is to come of the experience in the Great Central Sun,[1] of spiraling to the center of the flame?

You have but glimpsed the Infinite and yet you have felt the pulsations of the Godhead. You have felt the movement of energy, the motion of the Mother. You have fulfilled in part the impetus of the soul, but you have felt an impetus that you have not fulfilled—that which is toward wholeness, toward freedom, and toward the creativity that you know exists within yet is not being released without.

Tapping the resources of a new consciousness is the joy of the alchemist in transition—of those who understand the all-chemistry of God taught by Saint Germain[2] as the day-by-day replacement of spirals of an older consciousness with spirals of a newer consciousness.

This is the meaning of the path of initiation—that increment by increment, line by line, the acceleration of consciousness, of light and light's determination, takes place within you.

Yes, I AM Maitreya. I stand before you in the golden flame of your own Cosmic Christ illumination.[3] I personify before you the image of your own Cosmic Christ awareness. I am, for a moment, the cosmic mirror, mirroring for you what you shall become. What you see in me is what you can be.

But some of you say, "I see nothing but the messenger standing before me." I tell you that your soul beholds, with the eyes of the soul, my aura, that which I have received from God by the process of initiation.

And therefore there is a transference to your souls this night of the image of the Cosmic Christ. There is the impression upon your subconscious and in your four lower bodies[4]—and, yes, in each and every chakra—of that Cosmic Christ consciousness that you are intended to be. And so the blueprint is transferred. Now, let us see how the filling in of the blueprint is a daily process.

The Cross as the Symbol of Initiation

Taking up the cross daily was the word of Jesus to describe the initiation of consciousness.[5] And the cross as the symbol of that initiation clearly marks the descent of Alpha as Spirit and the cross of Mater as the horizontal line.

And so you see that the cross of white fire goes ever before you as the sign of your own I AM THAT I AM,[6] as the fiery, flaming flame that will not be quenched. It is the going before you of those angelic presences who mark the path of initiation.

Chelas[7] entering the path of the ascension[8] know that many have gone before them to clear the way for their coming, and many will come after them because they have elected to take the initiations of the sacred fire.

And so you are standing at the nexus of the cross of life. And by standing there, by being willing to be the crystallization of the God flame, you are making possible the ascension of those who will come after you, and you are making possible the God-realization, the ongoingness of hierarchy[9] of those who have gone before.

And so there is a cosmic moment for each and every soul—a moment when that soul is on the cross of life, is bearing the karma for a planet and a people, is working out the karma of individual destiny, passing through the dark night of the soul and the dark night of the Spirit,[10] being required by the law of being to sustain a flame at the convergence of the spirals of the Father-Mother God. And in that converging of the spirals there is the opportunity to ratify Being, to make permanent the atom of Self.

You Are a Link in the Chain of Cosmic Consciousness

I AM Maitreya, and I AM on the cross of Cosmic Christ awareness. That *is* my position in hierarchy. Would you also define your position in hierarchy?

You are hierarchy where you are. You are a link in the chain of cosmic consciousness,[11] and through you pass the energies of life from higher evolutions to lesser evolutions. As you fulfill your role as a dispenser of cosmic light, souls are nourished on the Path.[12]

It is a fact of life and of hierarchy that unless you, the hierarch, rise in the higher arch of being, souls dependent upon you karmically and in their dharma and in their solar blueprint will not rise.

Do you wonder why the teeming masses of Terra do not rise? Do you wonder why they are in rebellion and why they organize revolutions against the elite?

It is because, you see, within their soul they realize that those who are above them in the social strata are responsible for keeping open the way of life. You must be the open door that no man can shut.[13] You must be the open door whereby others who are dependent upon your flame, your God-realization, might also initiate spirals of creativity and realize their awareness of God.

The Initiation of the Cycles of the Heart

The way of fulfillment is not the superstate, for the superstate can never fulfill the yearnings of the masses to be free, to be one in the flame of God. Not in the state and not in a material religion, not in this or that philosophy, not in this or that economic policy, but through the initiation of cycles of the heart will the multitudes come into the awareness of God.

This is the meaning of the feeding of the multitudes and the pleading of the Master, "Feed my sheep. Simon Bar-jona, lovest thou me more than these, more than these stones, more than these fishes, more than this bread? Lovest thou me more than all outer manifestation? Feed my sheep."[14]

In order to feed the sheep, you must draw from the Good Shepherd the energies of life, the wherewithal to nourish the flock. Feeding the sheep, dispensing the bread and the fish to the five thousand, is a demonstration of hierarchy whereby through your heart chalice and your Christ consciousness[15] there is delivered unto the flock increments of science and of knowledge and of love and of abundance and of the energies necessary for the sustainment of the body temple.

The urgency of the message comes as you understand the ongoing nature of hierarchy. Each successive one who holds the shepherd's crook—each one who holds the authority for church, for state, for a group of souls or for one or two—must understand that unless this feeding, this nourishing of life, this giving, this releasing of energy is fulfilled, there will be a blockage of the flow of the creative life force and a stopping of the action of hierarchy.

The Loss of Contact with the Inner Flame and the Inner Guru

Why do you not hear of hierarchy and of the ascended masters and of those masterful beings who are administering to life on Terra and in these systems of worlds?

You do not hear of hierarchy because those in control of government and religion and science have denied hierarchy and the passing of the torch from generation to generation, from ascended beings to unascended beings. And therefore there is on this darkened star a blockage of the energies of flow and thus the consequence of disintegration, disease, death and dying, despair and despondency. This is the result of mankind's loss of contact with the inner flame and the inner guru, the loss of contact with the hierarchy of light.

Understand, then, that when you break the chain of hierarchy you cut the tie to the Sun behind the sun. You cut off the flow of a cosmos and the energies must circumvent that flame, that presence, that planetary orb. And these energies move on in the cosmic scheme, contacting only those souls who are part of this chain of cosmic consciousness.

You are all a part of hierarchy if you will only think. You have your respective positions in your family, in your schools, in your businesses, in your professions, and you are aware of those who excel in the way you have chosen and you are aware of your own excellence. You are aware of talents that you can impart to others and talents that must be refined and perfected before they can be passed on, which is your rightful responsibility in the demonstration of the sacred labor.[16]

The Individualization of the God Flame

The cutting off of the opportunity for the realization of the God consciousness in the crown, in the third eye, and in the throat chakra is the denial of God-reality, as Above, so below. It is the cutting off of the leadership of the individual and of society.

And so when mankind take the law of equality and misuse it, they destroy hierarchy. Indeed it is true that all men and women are created equal, but equality ceases the moment the individual begins the exercise of free will. By free will that flame is manifest as vice or virtue, as the highest or the lowest in the potential of man and of woman.

And therefore you are not equal in attainment in this moment. You are not equal in the cycles of God-realization. You are not equal in the application of the flame or in your talents or in their realization. And if you were, how monotonous life would be!

There is no such thing as equality, for hierarchy is the ladder of cosmic consciousness wherein all the sons and daughters of God assume their position and their role as instruments for the release of a facet of the mind of God.

When a society ceases to pattern its laws and its institutions after the laws of hierarchy, when there is the leveling of all as the masses, then the opportunity to be a link in the chain, to be an individual God flame, is no more.

This is the depression of the soul—when the soul realizes that its opportunity for the individualization of the God flame in hierarchy has been cut off by the state, by the church, by the economy, by the laws, by systems of taxation, by systems contrived by a humanitarian consciousness that seek the values of humanism and a humanistic ideal.

The Golden-Age Society and the Right to Rule

Mankind cannot base their society on man but on God and God-realization. They cannot center hierarchy, initiation, and attainment in the human ideal but in the divine ideal, for the divine ideal is the cause behind the effect that is the human ideal.

And therefore society, if it is to be a golden-age society, must return to that level of the understanding of hierarchy wherein the initiates of the Buddha and of the Christ are those who are given the right to rule—those who manifest the law of cosmic consciousness, who have the right, the divine right to declare, "I AM the Law! I AM the Word incarnate!" This is the divine right of kings and queens.

And who are the kings and queens? Those who have raised the energies of Father and of Mother to the perfect balance of the life force.

And who are the priests and priestesses? Those who have tended the altars of the hearts of humanity. Those who have kept the flame of life on behalf of their sisters and brothers on the Path. These have the right to minister unto the flock, to break the bread and offer the Communion cup—not those charlatans, not the wolves in sheep's clothing who have taken their studies and their courses in the schools of philosophy and theology and who come to pursue the profession as a trade, as a means of livelihood instead of as the calling of the Holy Spirit.

And who are they who have the right to be called the scientists of the age? Who are they who have the right to hold in their hands life and death but those who have mastered the flame of precipitation, those who have come forth as alchemists of the sacred fire, who have proven their responsibility to work with nuclear energies and spiritual energies and the energies of life in the heart of the atom and in the heart of the I AM Presence? [See inset "The Chart of Your Divine Self," pp. 104–09.]

To whom have you entrusted the secrets of science? Who holds the power to unleash nuclear warfare in your society—those who have attainment, or the madmen who have come again from Atlantis and Lemuria who have reinstated themselves in the seat of authority in institutions of science and at the heads of government, who have become the demigods?

Mankind worship the scientists instead of the flame, and they do not recognize the irresponsibility of those who experiment with energies and who release the by-products of nuclear fission into the body of the earth for the pollution of the planes of Mater.

Children of the light, sons and daughters of God, you have the right to rule when you are centered in the flame! You have the right to be ruled by those who are centered in the flame! And you have the right to overthrow, by the mandate of the electorate, those individuals who usurp the God flame, who displace your Christ consciousness and your free will by the carnal mind, by their cults of Satanism!

Though they know it not, they are Satanists. For they have inverted the star of man's being and exalted the carnal mind in the place of the Christ. And so the intellect becomes king and queen and priest and priestess—a mockery of the flame of the Mother. And this was the desecration of that flame that caused the sinking of Lemuria—when the outer shell and the mechanization of that flame became the replacement for the divine ideal.

I Extend the Cup of Opportunity

I AM Maitreya, and I was with the Ancient of Days, Sanat Kumara.[17] I was with Lord Buddha and the Christed One. I was with the Elohim in the creation of worlds. I too can declare,

"Before Abraham was, I AM."[18] And I have seen the rise and fall of civilizations. I have seen the potential for the golden age and I have seen the breaking of the cup—the dashing of the cup of consciousness into a thousand pieces.

I have seen the ruination of the matrix of the Mother. I have seen the desolation of the temple. I have seen the winds of the Holy Spirit increase unto the utter destruction, by the action of the Destroyer, Shiva, of all of the miscreations of mankind.

I want to tell you that I have also seen individually your comings and your goings. I have seen your risings and your fallings on the path of life. And so you have come once again to be enlightened. Let me warn you—you have been enlightened before!

I have come to you before with a cup of wisdom. You have taken that cup, and then because of the failure to surrender ambition and pride you have fallen again. You have become drunk with the knowledge of the sacred fire! You have used it to elevate the ego and the lesser self! Had you used it to elevate the Divine Ego and the Higher Self, you would not be sitting in these halls. You would not be here seeking again that sacred energy. You would be with me an ascended master, a teacher of mankind.

It Is Time for the Soul to Return to the God Consciousness

Yes, you have had opportunity again and again, and justice and mercy and the full complement of the Law. I will not tell you sweet stories when it is time to hear the truth and to face the truth! For many, in this conclusion of an age, it is the last time. It is the opportunity, finally, to determine: Will you take this cup of light, this cup of cosmic consciousness? Will you use it, once and for all, to make your way back to the heart of God, to release only the glory of God in your being? Will you take it, then?

I extend the cup once again. For some it will come again. For others they will face the judgment before they have another opportunity to have the cup of enlightenment.

Take seriously, then, the path of initiation. Understand that you are old souls—souls who have been evolving, in some cases, hundreds of thousands and millions of years. It is time for the soul to return to the God consciousness. And in this space you have opportunity to do just that—to apply the teachings of the Divine Mother,[19] to take the thread of hierarchy, to take that thread and to wind it on the spool of being. Let it wind around the spine as Kundalini fires.[20] Let it wind around that spool for the spinning of the thread and then the weaving of the garment—the wedding garment of God.

Take the teaching but recognize your responsibility in taking the teaching. For some have come before you and have taken the radiation, the light, the energy of the masters and the Mother. They have run with the torch, and in their running they have forgotten the Source. They have taken the torch, claimed it as their own, and elevated themselves before the surrender of the ego and in place of the guru.

Seek to Be God-Taught

Seek to be God-taught and God will call you when you are ready to be a teacher with the World Teachers[21]—to be God-taught, to reinforce light within you, to be all one in the flame. Let this be your goal and your daily striving.

And forget not the invocations to light, for many who come after you are totally dependent upon those invocations as their only source of the God flame. [See inset "Decrees & the Science of the Spoken Word," pp. 110–15.] For they have not heard of the flame that burns on the altar of the heart. They have not heard of the Christ Self or of the I AM THAT I AM. [See inset "The Chart of Your Divine Self," pp. 104–09.] The door has not been open to them for cosmic flow and therefore they are the sheep who must be fed daily and hourly for the fulfillment of the divine plan.

Sons and daughters of God, I challenge you to take the mantle of responsibility to fulfill your divine plan. I challenge you to call to me so that I might come, by your free will, to initiate spirals of God consciousness within you.

I challenge you to test hierarchy, to test the Brotherhood, to test the teaching and the teacher. I challenge you to accelerate consciousness for the glory of God in manifestation. And when I see manifest in you the action of the Law by your devotion, by your dedication, I will match that manifest action. I will add my momentum to your own. And so point by point, line by line as you persevere, I will reinforce the flame that you garner.

I AM in the central sun of your heart the awareness of your cosmic consciousness.

I AM Maitreya of the flame.

October 10, 1975
San Francisco, California

*I shall come to you.
Heed my voice and my word,
and know the voice of the Good Shepherd
of your own Christ Self.
Know the voice of your own Christ Self!
Prepare the way and the channels of consciousness.
For behold, I come quickly.*

CHAPTER 2

The Exchange of the Cosmic Cubes

I AM the Buddha of the sun of your heart. I AM the Buddha who lives in the light of love. I live only where love is fulfilled in the fulfilling of the Law, and where love remains unfulfilled, I withdraw. This is the law of octaves. This is the law of cosmic consciousness—that those in hierarchy who personify cosmic consciousness may only be where cosmic consciousness is personified.

With what crystal quality the concepts of truth are defined! With what geometry the equation of being is revealed! Line upon line, as the formation of the crystals of fire within you and within Mater, so are the lines of God's consciousness. These lines are the fire of the mind of God. And not a particle of dust, not a particle of human emotion can cling to these lines that compose the forcefield of God-awareness within you.

By gazing on the dust, on the particles of energy misqualified, you lose contact with the blueprint, with the fiery forcefield, with the mandala of being. And when you lose contact you lose the thread of hierarchy, and for that moment you are out of contact with the Great White Brotherhood.[1]

By your own consciousness you break the thread. By your own consciousness you weave the thread. Again and again you weave the thread, only to break it again by allowing your attention to be diverted, to amplify the substance that is unreal.

And so I come. I come in the flame of Cosmic Christ-awareness. I come to mend the broken threads in the delicate lace of the veil of your virginity. I come to reestablish the virgin consciousness. I come to mend the flaws. I must have your cooperation.

I have sent my angels into your rooms. I have sent my angels to mend the wedding garment.[2] They are expert seamstresses. They come. They come with golden threads of light. They come with the energies of your own causal body[3] and of dispensations. They come in answer to your call, but through misunderstanding and misapplication there is the failure to cooperate.

Dispensations Received and Lost

Imagine your own exasperation if you were to find yourself sewing diligently on the wedding garment, sewing on the garment of the bride of the soul, and for hours and hours you are meticulously working on that garment, embroidering the delicate flowers, the roses and the violets and the forget-me-nots and the lilies.

Enter, then, the Fallen One,[4] who tears from you the garment, who undoes the threads. And in your dismay and in your fear and in your shock, you are motionless, petrified, and you watch all your work being undone in that moment.

Now you understand the angels of Maitreya who come. They see how you tear and dash the precious matrix of the light of the Mother in the unkind word, in the release of sarcasm, in the conversation that is not the affirmation of truth. And when you have finished your discord and when you have given full vent to your emotions and all is then disturbed, there is a loss of energy and you are drained of your allotment of light. And then you sleep or you rest. So with the coming of the Holy Spirit—the balancing of energies with the giving again of your invocations—a new equilibrium is established and the angels begin again.

Precious hearts, I am giving to you an attempt at a graphic presentation of what has taken place in your world hundreds and thousands of times, over and over again. Through past ages you have been given these dispensations for initiation, and then by breaking the thread of contact[5] again and again you have lost the dispensation, and the angels have been forced to withdraw by the law of octaves.

And so the cycles have passed—decades and centuries and entire embodiments—wherein you have not had the visitation of these angels of Maitreya weaving the wedding garment, weaving with your soul and your Christ consciousness that garment that you must wear in the hour of initiation.

Choose What You Will Wear to the Marriage Feast

You cannot come to the altar at Luxor,[6] to the altar of this retreat, without a portion of the wedding garment. For the hierarchies of light cannot take from you that human consciousness, which you would be relieved of, unless there is another consciousness that you can wear. They will not strip you of your garments and leave you bare, standing there naked before the world, before the forces of destruction and the forces of construction, for you would be vulnerable.

And therefore we must leave you with some clothing to wear, even if it be the tattered garments of your own ego. Understand that even this forcefield, in all of its density, affords the soul some measure of insulation against the fallen ones.

And therefore you must choose what you will wear to the marriage feast, what you will wear to the Supper of the Lord. And by your choosing you will either be taken into the Holy of Holies[7] or cast into outer darkness, where there is weeping and gnashing of teeth.[8]

Therefore my angels stand ready again to repair the thread

and to repair the garments of those who sincerely apply the Law and pursue God-harmony as the ultimate expression of divinity—harmony that consumes all misuses of the light of the Mother. So in the stillness of harmony, the alchemy is performed.

And so we have created the equation that you call Summit University[9]—a place for the meeting of the soul and the Spirit for a period, for cycles of transmutation, for cycles of God-realization. I am come to initiate, and I make known to you the requirements of initiation.

The Exchange of the Cubes of Consciousness

Now I shall describe the initiation that I shall perform for you in the hour and in the coming of the flame and in the coming of your surrender.

It is the exchange of the cubes of consciousness—the cube of the Macrocosm of the Cosmic Christ and the cube of the microcosm of your self-awareness.[10]

And when this initiation takes place, you will visualize yourself standing in two cubes of fire. The cubes meet at the heart. They dissect the heart at the point of the threefold flame.[11] The threefold flame rises into the upper cube, and its energies are projected into the lower cube. You are enveloped in these cubes.

At the point of initiation (if you have qualified for initiation when the point is present), then I will, as the consciousness of the Cosmic Christ, fill the upper cube with my momentum and my light, reinforced by the momentum of your own Christ-awareness and your own I AM Presence. And the maximum consciousness of God that your chakras can contain—the heart, the throat, the third eye, and the crown—will be anchored there and multiplied again by the light of the Cosmic Christ.

Then in the moment of initiation there will be an exchange

of cosmic cubes. The upper cube will descend; the lower cube will ascend. The upper cube will absorb and transmute and dissolve by the fire of the Spirit impurities in the lower cube. And the lower cube will be impressed with the momentums of Spirit, and that forcefield will be held. And then the exchange will occur again. And the upper cube that has descended will rise again to the place of the focus of Spirit, and the lower cube that has ascended will descend again. This is the controlled exchange of Macrocosm and microcosm in the forcefield of the Cosmic Christ. It is the magnetizing of God consciousness in the seven levels of being.

I Release to You the Formula for Your Initiation

I shall come to you. Heed my voice and my word, and know the voice of the Good Shepherd of your own Christ Self. Know the voice of your own Christ Self! Prepare the way and the channels of consciousness. For behold, I come quickly![12]

Behold, I come quickly, and in the twinkling of the eye of God there will be the dissolving, by the action of the sacred fire, of that substance that is less than God-desire. It is the energy of God within you desiring to be free! Now let us see if you will *let* it be free and claim your freedom in the Cosmic Christ consciousness.

I AM who I AM. I AM where I AM. I AM only where the devotee is sealed in the law of love. I release to you the formula for your initiation. It is locked in your own heart flame.

Guard the flame!
Guard the flame!
Guard the flame!

October 19, 1975
La Tourelle
Colorado Springs, Colorado

*I AM Maitreya, initiator of souls,
and I am always watching
for the soul who is ready
to be initiated in the unexpected.
This requires flexibility,
being accustomed to the wind of the
Holy Spirit blowing to and fro.*

CHAPTER 3

Expect the Unexpected

I come to fill your hearts with mercy and compassion, with the pink and the violet of the amethyst egg and ascension's flame anchored therein.

I would touch your hearts through the Mother,* that your hearts might be filled to overflowing with that balm of mercy and compassion so needed by the world in the coming year and always, and so needed by you as you move among mankind dispensing the light of God.[1]

In order to enter the Path, souls need forgiveness and love. By extending the love and the forgiveness of God, you prepare the way for their acceptance of our offering as the teaching, as the initiation. Always remember that love must be without dissimulation. It must be given freely, abundantly, equally to all who come to you for assistance.

And when you have given love and more love, extend also mercy. As the flame of forgiveness that becomes the adornment of the soul praying in the temple—the robe of the devotee, the shawl of the humble—so is mercy a garment to be worn, signifying the atonement of the Mediator,[2] the intercession of the Mother, and the dispensations of hierarchy.

---

*The messenger

You Will Not Be Initiated in That Which You Expect to Be Initiated In

I come, then, to the place where mankind are found in life, needing to be washed clean, needing the flow of the waters of the Word, needing to know that they are loved by compassion and compassion's flame.

I AM Maitreya, initiator of souls, and I am always watching for the soul who is ready to be initiated in the unexpected. This requires flexibility, being accustomed to the wind of the Holy Spirit blowing to and fro, rearranging the garment of mercy and requiring continual adjustment and therefore continual openness to the flame and to flexibility.

You will not be initiated in that which you expect to be initiated in. I can assure you of that! I can assure you that you may study and prepare and give your decrees,[3] and just when you are all decreed up on illumination's flame, you will be tested in the emerald ray. And in that moment when you realize that you have been caught either empty-handed or red-handed, as the case may be, you must say to yourself:

> *I AM ready because God in me is ready. I AM ready because the white fire of initiation's flame contains the allness of God and every good and perfect gift.*
>
> *I AM ready, LORD. Do with me what you will, but I AM ready to answer the call, to fulfill the requirements of hierarchy. I have asked for initiation, and I will take it when it comes.*

The True Chela Is Never Off Guard

And so you can anticipate initiations, but somehow they come when you are least prepared and off guard. And yet how can we say this of the true chela [disciple], for the true chela is never off guard, waking or sleeping. This is a preparation for initiation.

It is wakefulness. It is being alert. It is expecting the Bridegroom at the midnight hour.[4] It is expecting the coming of the Keeper of the Scrolls[5] or the vials of the seven last plagues.[6] It is setting yourself as a diamond set in Mater, set in the very hills of the human consciousness and saying, "Let all the world and all of heaven and earth come to me! I AM set and I AM ready!"

Remember Jesus as he saw the multitudes representing all aspects of the human consciousness. And seeing their consciousness, he went up into a mountain. And when he was set in the Christ consciousness of the Cosmic Christ, he called his disciples unto him and he taught them, giving them the Beatitudes, blessing the multitudes, and teaching the end of that state of consciousness. The meek, the humble, the peacemakers, the poor in spirit—all were aspects of the multitudes.[7]

But he did not begin to teach until he was set in the Christ consciousness. And yet you say, "Jesus was always set in the Christ consciousness," which is true. But there is a dialing of that consciousness, a focusing of a spectrum, whether as a concentrated band in the chakras or as a wide band including the aura of a planet.

"Getting set" means getting ready for the task at hand. It does not mean that you are off guard. It means that you are on guard in the white flame of purity, ready to adjust yourself to whatever is the need and requirement of the hour.

We Observe the Tests Coming as the Rolling of a Reel of Ticker Tape

I trust that you will not consider these words too simple or too remote, for I assure you that they are not remote but very close to your heart, to my heart, and to the heart of God. For we observe daily the activities of the chelas and we observe the tests coming as the rolling of a reel of tape, of ticker tape. And we see the punching of the grand computer of God's own mind releasing the specific formulas of initiation according to the cycles of personal and planetary karma, and we see those who pass their tests and those who fail their tests.

Some chelas fail their tests, not knowing that they have been tested, which is the greatest tragedy of all. Others fail the test, knowing that they are being tested and choosing not to pass the test. This too is a tragedy, but at least they have exercised free will. When you are in the state of ignorance, it is like being asleep and having a wave of the Great Central Sun pass over you and not knowing that the wave has passed.

I Trust That You Will Allow Me to Teach You

I come in the flame of the new year. I come in the flames of faith and hope and charity. I come to overshadow those who with Jesus would be the Christed ones. I am ready to release the mantras to your soul.

I am ready to take you into the Royal Teton Retreat[8] again, those of you who have attended our Christmas seminar there on initiation.[9] I am ready to instruct you in the mind of the Buddha—the planetary Buddha, the personal Buddha, the cosmic Buddha.

I am ready, and I trust that you will allow me to teach you, for the ascended masters have the same passion as the Mother to transfer that consciousness to embodied souls. We are determined to plant the rod of light and the cones and the cubes within the subconscious of those who make themselves ready.

**I Have Come with a Very Special Increment
of Light for Your Heart**

I have come, as I have told you, with a very special increment of light for your heart. It is a soothing action and a mellowing action.

Where some of you have records of hardness of heart there can take place, if it is your will, a softening, a tenderness, the filling of your heart with such mercy as to make you more supple to the flow of love to all mankind.

You know that I am a master of the crown chakra and of wisdom's flame. Then understand that I deem it important for the clearing of the way in the heart, for the coming of the light of the crown, that you should be found to be the most merciful and the most compassionate of all people.

This does not mean that you allow souls to indulge their human consciousness. The very foundation of mercy and compassion is the grid of the will of God. It is the outline that is firm. And in the firmness of that chalice, love and mercy can flow and yet not be compromised by those who would flaunt the Law.

Let the eye of the sons and daughters of God be a tender regard for all life, and behind the tender regard let there be the piercing brilliance of the will of God, of the eye of Morya.[10]

Love and Mercy Come in Many Forms

Do you not understand that to gaze into Serapis's eyes is to see disciplined love[11] and that many times, although the outer man rebels, the inner soul is so grateful to receive love in the form of a discipline that will propel the soul into the likeness of its Maker. Love and mercy take many forms. The casting out of twin flames[12] from the circle of oneness called the garden of paradise* was a supreme act of mercy and compassion and yet was the sternness of the Law.

Rather than allow these twin flames to pass through the second death[13] for their sins, the LORD God provided opportunity for the return to paradise lost. And what if that opportunity be

---
*the Garden of Eden

the toiling by the sweat of the brow, the pain, and the experience of outer darkness? Is this not calculated by the most intense ray of compassion to propel souls back to the center of that garden of wisdom?

The Edenic consciousness is the goal of your life. You are living on a planetary home sustained by love and mercy in order to give you the opportunity to return through the open door of your Christ consciousness to the white-fire core,[14] to the Tree of Life,[15] and to the tree of the knowledge of Good and Evil, where you will have restored your immaculate conception of absolute perfection.

Going back to the Garden of Eden is a step-by-step process of initiation. Each erg of energy spilled upon the ground must be recaptured in love.

Karma Is Mercy and Compassion That Would Draw the Soul Back to God

You are coming nearer and nearer to the Edenic bliss as you worship the I AM Presence, as you see that Presence as the Tree of Life. As you sit under that tree and meditate in the Christ Self and in the flame, you are surrounded by cherubim keeping the way of the Tree of Life. The guardian action of the angelic hosts is the action of the flame, is the action of mercy and of compassion.

I AM that light which lighteth every man and woman that cometh into the world.[16] I AM that light of the Holy of Holies and I would transfer that light to you, that portion for your return.

Mankind have thought that the concept of the Fall was mere allegory. How can they think this when their souls hold the memory of paradise lost? How can they think this when they see themselves aged, decrepit, subject to disease, incomplete, burdened by karma and unhappiness?

Surely God did not will these conditions. Surely all who are fair toward God and self must recognize that individual responsibility is the only factor in present circumstances and conditions. This is the responsible teaching. This is the action of the Great Central Sun Magnet.[17] This is compassion.

For unless these conditions come upon mankind to teach them the errors of their ways, how can they learn that fire is hot, that ice is cold? How can they learn the thousand-and-one facts about cause-and-effect sequences? How can they learn?

And so karma is not punishment. Karma is mercy and compassion that *would* preserve the soul in eternity, that *would* draw the soul back to God and therefore that must teach the soul the way of Christ-mastery.

I Would Make of You True Initiates on the Path

I am initiating you in love, that love might become the magnet of your God-desire—God in you desiring to be whole, God in you desiring to be the fullness of Christ peace, God in you desiring to be perfection in the Law. I AM the fullness of that love that is the fulfillment of every need, human and divine.

I would make of you, as quickly as possible, true initiates on the Path, true disciples of the Christ and of Buddha. I would make you, as quickly as possible, the authority for your life and for your world. I would make you teachers of the children of God. I would make you instruments for the passing of the fires of regeneration.

I send forth the light of the resurrection flame! I send forth the light of the will of God! Now, if you would become all these things that I would have you become, you must accept the chastening of the fire, the intensification of the fire, and an accompanying discomfort as your atoms and molecules adjust to the fervent heat of God's love.

The Miracle of the Rebirth

And after you pass through this initiation of the fiery furnace with Shadrach, Meshach, and Abednego,[18] you will find yourself refired in the kiln of the mind of God—truly reborn in body and soul and spirit, in mind and heart. *Truly reborn.* And as you have heard, it is the rebirth that is the key to the expansion of the light and the teaching of the ascended masters.

Many of you have experienced the rebirth in part or in whole as you have made your way to Summit University. You have seen yourselves transformed. You have heard your families say, "Why, I just don't know you. You are a different person."

You have seen, then, the miracle of the rebirth. How do you think these things happen? Are you so immersed in light that you do not see that miracles are happening to ascended master chelas? And can you not see that if we are able through the Mother to dispense miracles to the chelas, that we can dispense miracles across the land, the sea, the sky, through elemental life,[19] through all mankind, then we can transform the governments and economies of the nations as quickly as we can transform a blade of grass, an elemental, a chela on the Path?

We have the formula and the alchemy. We need only the repository of the human soul. We need those in embodiment who will set themselves upon the mount of attainment and who will be set to give forth precisely the teaching and the flow and the Law and the energy that is necessary for the conveyance of the mantle of the entire Spirit of the Great White Brotherhood. This is our goal.

You who are initiates who count yourselves among the ranks of the Brotherhood and the servants of the Brotherhood, must envelop Terra in a blanket of sacred fire. The blanket must be anchored in the physical, and the only anchoring point is the flame within your heart. And when it is anchored there, it can be extended to every other chakra in your being until you become a blazing Sun of righteousness[20] and the fullness of the Law on earth as in heaven.

I Call My Chelas Home

I AM Maitreya. I call my chelas Home. I call the weary. I call those who have fallen from the Way. I call all who are there who would do the will of God and yet question the word of the Mother. I call to you and I say: I AM Maitreya in the Mother. Accept your initiations! Accept your calling!

Hear the call of hierarchy echoing from the Himalayas, echoing from the Royal Teton! Hear the call of hierarchies from out the Great Central Sun! Submit to the tasks at hand and call for your Christ-mastery to transmute the cause and core of the doubting of the Word, of the fear and trembling of the assignment, of the questioning of the Teacher. This is the age of the coming of the Buddha and the coming of the Mother. And the banners of Maitreya and of the Mother are flying over Terra.

Now, then, Christ Selves of each one assembled here, I call to you now to begin the intensification of the sphere of the Christ consciousness within the heart chakra. Begin to intensify the action of the threefold flame, for I, Maitreya, am come.

I salute you, each and every one, each Christed one. I salute the flame and the Godhead within you. I come, then, to add the momentum of my light so that each heart might have a right start, a kindling fire, a threefold flame, a matrix of the Mater, a matrix of the Buddha.

I come to give you a head start in this year, to give you opportunity to cast out every fear and anxiety, to cast out all agitation and accusation of the fallen ones, to go forth to the lost sheep of the house of Israel with the true knowledge of the Law and the Logos, of the prophets and the Christed ones, and of the Great Teams of Conquerors[21] from out the Great Central Sun.

O chelas of the flame, O Christ Selves of all, let us go forth together and convey to all life the magnet of the Great Central Sun! Let us do it! Let us do it! Let us do it together in his name!

In the name of the I AM THAT I AM, I salute the light within you, and I AM Maitreya.

December 31, 1975
Anaheim, California

*Drink of the elixir of love
and let love be the fullness
of the message of the sacred heart—
burning and expanding until you yourself
are consumed by all-consuming love,
and in that consummation
you realize the Self in higher and higher
spirals of being.*

CHAPTER 4

The Wooden Begging Bowl

Hail, O infinite fire of love! I send love arcing from the plane of Reality, where I AM, into the valleys and the mists of maya, where you seem to be but are not.

I reveal my face, face-to-face. I AM the lover of your soul. I AM the beloved, drawing you nearer and nearer to the goal of life, which is love. As you see me face-to-face, you remember the ancient mysteries and the Ancient of Days. Suddenly you remember your origin and the vastness of the void of reality, which contains the stars, the deities—angles of God's consciousness—and immediately you leave all and you run for the Sun. You run into the arms of the Sun and you keep on running and you keep on running. You run Home to love.

This is why God does not reveal himself fully, wholly, day by day. For so many would abandon the cares, the karma of this world, and the duty to be the dharma and the duty to open the way for all beings to live. And therefore the veil covers the reality of who you are so that the spirals of life may continue and God may realize himself as God even here below.

I AM the love magnet, drawing untold evolutions to the love-magnet center of life. I come to initiate your soul by love. I give to you, then, the token of my heart flame whereby you are seized as by Cupid's arrow, enamored of God, in love with God, and in search of only one embrace—the divine embrace, the everlasting embrace whereby you, no longer alone, are all One—nevermore to go out but only to be, to atone for all life, to bring love, to excel in love, exceed in love, expand in love, and thereby to realize the discipline that is required of the overcomer on the Path.

I Come for the Transfer of the Light of My Heart

Yes, I AM the Coming Buddha who has come. I have released my spiral in this age, and it is a wide spiral of love. I have surrounded you and every soul of light with a spiral that has become a geometric swaddling garment, a fohatic light for the All to become within you the One.

Blessed hearts, the path of initiation is only so that you might put on, increment by increment, the garment of the LORD and therefore retain identity. For if God were to bestow upon you the sacred-fire mystery all at once, you would become the self-dissolved in the Self. And only God, without the individualization of the flame of *you*, would remain. But you become the hierarchy. You become the keystone when you agree to pass, line upon line, through the initiations of the sacred fire.

I come, then, for the transfer of the light of my heart. And this night it is simply an intensification of God as love in your heart—a love for the *per-Son* of God, the personal manifestation of God that dwells concomitantly with the eternal Spirit. To be in love with a Person of God is to be assimilated by that Person and therefore to become that one—simple mystery of the buddhic path, simple mystery of the light. But I AM Maitreya. I AM the initiator of the love spiral.

The Begging Bowl of Consciousness

Now perceive the bowl of your consciousness hewn out of natural wood. Now see as I pour the elixir of love into the wooden bowl. Have you thought of yourself as the begging bowl? Have you thought of the carrying of the begging bowl as initiation on the Path, the key to the realization that man is a beggar before God and that when he ceases to be ashamed of that truth, then he will ask and receive the elixir of love?

In the secondary manifestation, the monk with the begging bowl must learn the perfection of indifference, for some deposit love in the bowl and others hatred. Those who deposit hatred despise and reject the Christ in the one who comes, and therefore they renounce in themselves the position of God and the opportunity of God to give unto God the fullness of the requirement of the hour.

Blessed ones, now in this cycle of the Coming Buddha who has come, all life on earth receives initiation hour by hour, day by day. Until my coming in the flame of the Cosmic Christ for this age, initiation was only for those who would seek and find the Guru. Now, with the acceleration and the compelling of the Law and the compelling of earth's evolutions into oneness with that law, none are exempt.

Lo, the day is at hand, and every lifestream must give accounting to the Guru Maitreya as to whether they will enter the mainstream of initiation of life or be found high and dry upon the shore without identification with the movement of God. I pray, then, that you will pray that every form of life on earth might reach for the next rung and the next rhythm in the movement of consciousness.

I Come That You Might Seek God as the Divine Lover of Your Soul

I ask you to pray for the deliverance of souls, for their salvation through Jesus Christ, through Gautama Buddha, through the I AM THAT I AM, through the message of God unto Mohammed, through the sayings of Confucius, Zarathustra, Melchizedek, Lao Tzu, and all who have carried the flame of Mother East and West. I ask you to pray that the deliverance of souls come quickly and that the manifestation of God consciousness on earth be the fulfillment of the realization of love and only love.

Hear the bubbling, crystal waters of the elixir of love that I pour carefully into your bowl. Your soul extends to me with outstretched hands now the wooden bowl of life. I pour into this hemisphere of self and I say to self, Drink ye all of it.[1] Drink of the elixir of love and let love be the fullness of the message of the sacred heart intensifying, burning within your heart—burning and expanding until you yourself are consumed by all-consuming love, and in that consummation you realize the Self in higher and higher spirals of being.

Love does not leave you where it finds you. Though you may be devastated by love, yet love, in stripping you of the guises and disguises of the former self, does propel you to that higher realm of consciousness where you are the lover, the beloved, the soul fused in the One.

I come, then, to initiate you in the love ray with Paul the Venetian, Chamuel and Charity, with Heros and Amora, and all Buddhas of infinite love.[2] I come that you might seek God as the divine Lover of your soul, that you might seek me as the personification of that Lover, that you might realize yourself as Mother, and in your meditation flow in and out of Maitreya as the stream seeking the vortex of light that is the ascension flame—seeking and finding the fulfillment of the soul and the Self by the spiral of the ascension that is the quintessence of God's love for all life.

And so the ascension, my beloved, is the consummation of our love. And in this marriage of your soul unto me, unto God, know the eternal bliss and the entering into the Home, the sacred Aum.[3]

The Fulfillment of Love in the Age of Aquarius

I AM Maitreya, sustaining the flood tide of love. As you think upon me, visualize the moment of my coming. When you are with your wooden begging bowl held out to me, know the opportunity of the soul to make the transition from the beggar to the prince, and so to know, to reign in life as the beloved son, the beloved daughter.

Beloved ones, meditate upon the movement of the flow of the bubbling elixir of life filling the wooden bowl of consciousness. See me as I am depicted before you in the ancient statue that bears my name and my flame and my Electronic Presence.[4]

Visualize the Coming Buddha coming into your life, always with the initiation of love. Drink in love, be filled with love, and sustain this love that we share in the very midst of the hatred that sets itself against the fulfillment of love in the age of Aquarius.

Now, then, by the love that I impart, be the focal point for the transmutation, the consuming of war that comes from hatred, of prejudice that comes from hatred, of anti-Christ, anti-God that is the hatred of the Self—self-annihilation, the hatred of the little child, of the unborn, of the mother and the father and the Spirit.

The Eternal Christ, Incarnate as the Word in Many Sons and Daughters, Is the Self of God

Blessed ones, the annihilation of the Person of God is the ultimate hatred of the Fallen One. For the sin of the Fallen One is the refusal to bend the knee and to confess the name of the Cosmic Christ in Maitreya, in Jesus, in Krishna, in Christos, in your eternal Christ Self.

Therefore understand that the lie of the denial of the personification of God originated in the pride of the Evildoer, who would not worship the Son of God but who made himself equal with God, and only upon the basis of a pride-filled equality would the Evildoer give homage to God himself, almost as a patrimony, as a condescension.

Blessed ones, he who does not recognize the Holy Child as God and does not worship the God within the child denies the LORD God himself. For which one of you will acknowledge anyone who denies your offspring while saluting yourself?

Your offspring is yourself. The eternal Christ, incarnate as the Word in many sons and daughters, is the Self of God. Those who know not the Christ are as pagans, as idolaters, and they cut themselves off from the eternal One. For by that denial of the love of the only begotten Son and the love of God for the soul of humanity in sending that Son, they have therefore lost the contact with the threefold flame of their own divinity, which contains Father, Son, and Holy Spirit.

Know Me as I AM—the Initiator of All Levels and Planes of Christ Consciousness

I AM Maitreya. I stand before you in the fullness of my stature. As I confirm myself to your inner eye as the personification of God, I open the door for you to stand upon the platform of life as the personification of the Christ, to be the open door for that selfsame realization in all humanity. And therefore I must declare myself the Person of God, else deny forevermore your capacity to be the Son.

I have shared my communion cup of love. I have filled your beggar's bowl. And therefore you are no longer the beggar in life but the inheritor, the joint heir with the universal Christ.[5] Expand your Christ Self-awareness from the point of the heart to the point of Jesus Christ, to the point of Gautama Buddha, and know me as I AM—the initiator of all levels and planes of Christ consciousness.

I call, then, unto the twelve tribes of Israel. I send the lifeline of the pure Son of God and I say to all: Worship the Son, for only by worshipping the Son can you become the Son. This is the eternal message sent from the Father, which I confirm to your soul with the nearness of his heartbeat and his very breath.

I AM in you, Maitreya, the Coming Buddha who has come to call you Home to love.

December 3, 1977
San Francisco, California

*I encourage you, then,
to meditate deeply upon the great sphere
of my cosmic consciousness,
to penetrate the deeper mysteries of life
and to not be satisfied with
surface appearances.*

CHAPTER 5

Find Your Way Back to Me

God standeth in the congregation of the mighty; he judgeth among the gods.
How long will ye judge unjustly, and accept the persons of the wicked? Selah.
Defend the poor and fatherless: do justice to the afflicted and needy.
Deliver the poor and needy: rid them out of the hand of the wicked.
They know not, neither will they understand; they walk on in darkness: all the foundations of the earth are out of course.
I have said, Ye are gods; and all of you are children of the most High.
But ye shall die like men, and fall like one of the princes.
Arise, O God, judge the earth: for thou shalt inherit all nations.

~ Psalm 82

Children of my heart, I come in the love of the Cosmic Christ for your souls, for your souls' advancement on the path of initiation. For you see, in the very nucleus of the God consciousness of the Cosmic Christ is the seed-awareness of every living soul, and within that seed is the deep desiring of God for the return of the soul who has gone out of the way of wholeness.

And therefore we do contain the intensity of God's desiring for initiation, for by testing and the adding unto the soul of an increment of light because of the victorious passing of the test, there is added unto the soul the increment of our consciousness whereby that soul may increase God's awareness of that desire that he contains for the soul.

Do you see, beloved ones, that one must contain within oneself an element of that seed in order to have even the desire for initiation?

You must be of God and of that Cosmic Christ. That seed within your soul, then, responds to the desiring of God. Within the seed is the memory, the ancient memory recorded there of the origin of being in God. Only through that memory can the Lord God transmit the desire.

The Fallen Ones Have Determined to Destroy the Soul's Desiring for God

Beloved ones, did you know that the fallen ones who have moved against the souls of light upon this planet know that locked in the memory of the seed of every soul is the God consciousness of the inner experience in the Beginning in Alpha and Omega?

And therefore do you know, beloved ones, that these fallen ones have determined to destroy the soul's desiring for God? For by this they have contrived to take from the Path millions who are held in the balance in this hour.

How have they determined to do this? You need but look around you. They have created, East and West, a civilization based on the desire for myriad things—circumstances, powers, controls, entertainments, conquests. Beloved ones, the forcefields of desire and the desiring of the human consciousness are as a legion of demons.

Now, you have heard of the erasing of the memory of the brain by the process of lobotomy. What have the fallen ones further determined to do? They have determined to destroy within the very brain itself—the physical brain, the physical mechanism that is the instrument of the mind of God through the crown and the third-eye chakra—the ability for it to hold and to make contact with the memory that is stored and locked in the seed of the soul.

They cannot destroy that nucleus of light except the individual surrender his soul unto the fallen ones by agreeing in the way with the Adversary[1] through sympathy or through rebellion. But, as you see, many souls have not rebelled against God nor are they sympathetic to evil, and therefore the tampering with the soul will not work with those souls.

And so the innocent victims of the children and the youth are those who are receiving the greatest onslaught of the tampering with the brain cells through that which has come forth out of the pit—the rock music, the drug culture, the misuse of sexual energies. But more than that, beloved ones, by tampering with and manipulating the DNA chain, the fallen ones have determined that not-too-distant generations will be born without those cells within the brain that are the necessary contact with the chakras and with the soul.

The proposition on the council tables of the false hierarchy in this very era is to determine by outer and inner programming that the outer person will no longer have contact with the inner Person, that the glorious temple of the four lower bodies made by the Lord God should no longer be an instrument for the sensitivity of the soul, for the penetration of other octaves. And therefore they have planned a robot race.

Though the children of the light are not of the origin of the fallen ones, if the fallen ones can successfully cut off the individual's contact with his own solar awareness through the soul chakra, with his own heart flame through the heart chakra, with the mind of God through the crown and with all levels of his mighty consciousness, they then will have individuals who have the momentum of light and of karma and of evolution cut off from the land of the living, from the realm of First Cause.[2]

The Madness of the Mad Scientists and the Experimentation with the Seed of Life

You have heard of what I would consider eerie descriptions of beings from outer space manning flying saucers, resembling half-animal, half-human grotesque forms and colors, resembling not in any way the divine manifestation of the son or the daughter of God. Beloved ones, throughout the vastness of a Matter cosmos the experimentation with the seed of life and with the egg of Omega has been, I tell you, beyond your comprehension.

Many of these flying saucers are manned by what you would term a slave race, a robot race, and they are programmed from various quarters and segments of the galaxy. Some of these are entirely man-made and some of them are the remaining vestiges of evolutions who have been deprogrammed and separated scientifically from their inner contact with God. Thus they are portrayed as having no feelings, no sense of longing or devotion for the family.

But the concept of the false hierarchy's discipline and attainment is the altogether scientific mind that is not considerate of any conditions of the human being, the human soul, the human evolution, with its joys and its sorrows and its ability to cry and to sing and to experience pain and to experience the transmutation of pain into the bliss of God.

Beloved ones, our messenger may not be here, nor may you, when ultimately these expressions are intended to be rampant upon the planetary body. Thus I release my word as a portion of sacred scripture for the Aquarian age, that you and your offspring and generations to come may read avidly and righteously out of the very Book of Life from whence these truths are taken.

The warning of the madness of the mad scientists is not only of the future but it is of the past, as they have manipulated energy for the sinking of continents and the distortion of life on Lemuria and Atlantis.

The Avant-Garde of Light of Earth's Evolutions Also Need to Plan for the Centuries

Those, then, who would be initiates of the sacred fire in the age of Aquarius must come to know the vastness of the mind of the Cosmic Christ that contains, as the Mediator of a cosmos, the complete awareness and the recordings of all experiments that have ever been made by souls of God with the uses of the energies of the Christ and of the sacred fire.

And therefore, approach the mind of the Cosmic Christ with the sense that you, the living soul, will put on the mantle of responsibility to stand with your own beloved Christ Self and the Christ Selves of earth's evolutions to bear the responsibility of dealing with and grappling with those individuals who have been planning not only the conquest of this world but of many worlds for centuries upon centuries. These individuals have manipulated their own karma, reincarnating again and again with one another of like frequency, cloning themselves, reproducing themselves, creating in the test tube those manifestations that can be controlled for their purposes.

If, then, the fallen ones usurping the mind of Christ plan not for decades but for centuries, would it not be wise on the part of the avant-garde of light of earth's evolutions to also plan for the centuries, to plan for the hour when those souls as children of God will study every word and measured beat of that which has come forth in this dispensation of this two-thousand-year cycle?

Beloved ones, whether it is the defense of America or of millions of souls destined to ascend from the planetary body, you must think in terms of decades, centuries, and millennia. Let us then see how the children of God and sons and daughters working with the angels may also evolve a plan and set in motion, from the great causal body of the Great Divine Director,[3] those safety measures, safeguards that will put electrodes of the Cosmic Christ in the way of the Evildoers.

You have heard the reading of Psalm 82. I have selected that psalm so that you would understand that David and those who were a part of the setting forth of those psalms knew well that there moved among mankind an ancient seed of darkness whom mankind referred to as "the wicked"—that this seed of darkness, committed unto the destruction of souls from its very inception, cannot be considered as though equal in any way with the children of God.

Have No Fear to Point the Finger of the Lord's Judgment

Perhaps it is in style not to accuse or to expose or to reveal truth and error. Well, beloved ones, I would not exactly say that the Cosmic Christ is in vogue on earth today. Those who desire to be popular are not so quick to point the finger and to isolate those who have embodied evil, preferring rather to indicate that all individuals are sincere, well motivated, and somehow—by the accidents of mathematics or luck or astrology—some individuals' works result in failure and evil and others in victory and God-good.

Well, as you know, there is no accident in cosmos, and that which is within the individual is that which expresses, "Ye shall know them by their fruits."[4]

Climb, then, the highest mountain, where you will see from that vantage point the several evolutions upon earth and where you will understand that he who seeks the attainment of the Cosmic Christ must not fear—as John the Baptist did not fear, as Jesus Christ did not fear—to point the finger of the LORD's judgment at those who are usurping the very life of the souls of God in science, in misuses of nuclear energy, in laboratory experiments that go all the way from the manipulation of the very coil of life itself in the DNA chain to those experiments upon the newborn babies and avatars.

Let those, then, who would have my initiation surrender now the desire for popularity. You will never be able to amass around you both souls of light and souls of darkness and have them agree with you and praise your offering, so you might as well choose the sort of souls with whom you will frequent on this earth.

For when you compromise, you will be found in the midst of the congregation of the compromisers, and you will have their plaudits for a while. But when you are without compromise and when you dip into the purity of the light and expose those who misuse the law and the government and the supply and the abundance of God—those who abuse the farmer, the laborer, the working man and woman, those who build America by the sweat of the brow and the labor of their bodies—when you find them abused by the false shepherds, fear not.

Do you remember that it was indeed John the Baptist who accused the then ruling member of Rome of the immorality within his marriage? Outspoken, outright, came John the Baptist, telling him it was not lawful for him to be married in the condition in which he was married.[5] Beloved ones, this cost John his head, but *not* his soul, *not* his ascension, *not* his integrity, *not* his honor!

You have heard a notable one in your midst accuse the American people of being afraid to die for a cause. Peculiar, is it not, when history has shown again and again that those who fear to defend their freedom and their path of initiation will lose their life, as Jesus said.[6]

There Is an Evolution of Light and an Evolution of Darkness Dwelling Side by Side

What is, then, the initiation of the Cosmic Christ? It is the direct line between you and the position you seek—the position of the power of the Godhead, the wisdom and the love to walk the earth wearing the robe of the prophets, the messengers, the teachers, and using that robe to cleave asunder the Real from the unreal, to be the manifestation of the judgment, and to care for the children of God who are not yet mature enough to understand this very simple condition of an evolution of light and an evolution of darkness dwelling side by side, having similar appearances and yet their works do go before them.

It requires the maturity to accept the consequences of such an understanding of life. The consequences are, beloved ones—when you admit that individuals have free will and therefore may embody evil—that you must choose. You must choose to be either the one or the other, [the light or the darkness,] and without compromise proceed to protect the little ones, who do not know the difference.

We have given through our messenger specific teachings in this very conference[7] to you who may not have understood why. It is because, beloved ones, you cannot fight and win a battle of Armageddon if you do not know your enemy. It is as simple as that.

It is not enough to know the enemy. You must know the *strategies* of that enemy. I have given you but one of the false hierarchy's strategies—its attempt to destroy the cell-memory of the brain.

Many of you know that in the psychiatric hospitals of the Soviet Union, these brain operations or the taking in of certain chemicals by the patients are designed to and have indeed accomplished this very thing—making souls of great light mere vegetables in a given lifetime. This, then, is not as far removed as you might think. And there are many other ways of manipulating a light generation away from the desire for God.

God Almighty Has Fed into the Soul of Light His Own Cosmic Designs

If you will look by contrast at the seed of the wicked [compared to the seed within the soul of light], you will find this singular character trait of the seed of the wicked—the total and absolute absence of desire for reunion with God.

This desire is not something that can be transplanted by mechanical or surgical means. It is the original seed of God with which he has endowed the soul. And because that seed is within the soul, the LORD God himself knows that the soul can and shall return according to the exercise of free will.

Very immediate, then, upon the agenda of the sons and daughters of God pursuing the initiations of Maitreya is to remove from the children of God all that tampers with their individual free will, such as the hypnosis of the mass media, such as the misuse of the educational institutions to program little children and older children, as well as university students, as though they were robots.

Beloved ones, God Almighty has fed into the soul and the chakras and the spheres of being his own cosmic designs of a cosmic geometry. In the sense of the Godhead, then, you, as the offspring of the Most High, are indeed programmed. But this is the programming of the Cosmic Christ whereby in every cell there is a memory, a desire, an order, a universe, and a programming for the very life of that cell and what it must accomplish within the given organ of the body.

Therefore, when you see before you beauty or the illustrations that the Mother prepares for your meditation, when you recite the Word of God, do not let the fallen ones come in with their projections and say, "You are being programmed. Beware! You are receiving hypnosis now."

Beloved ones, understand that the method of the ascended masters and of the Cosmic Christ is to give you, in the full conscious mind of your being, the opportunity to choose and to select what you will deposit within your temple. After all, each time you think or move or act or meditate, it is not necessary for you to engage in the original creative act of the cosmos. There are some things that bear repetition by the very ritual and movement of energy from the center of the atom to the periphery. This is not rote. It is a cosmic ritual of the seventh age, always the ritual of Father, Son, and Holy Spirit, and of the Cosmic Virgin.

You will notice that the fallen ones never taunt you with their message, "You are being programmed like a robot," when you are before your television screens, when you are in your motion-picture theaters, or when you are reading your daily papers. All is silent, for now *they* are the ones who are doing the programming and they are frightened when they see that through your own Christ-potential you become selective.

Your mind can discern and discriminate, and therefore you accept or you reject, you receive or you say, "You will not enter." This intelligent receiving of the energies of the universe is as it is intended. But beloved ones, your advertising is filled with subliminal energies, designs of pornography, designs to create a desire in you for a product, and people go on and on.

And so, you see, it is not quite cricket,* as they say, for the fallen ones to be free to program the children of God. Yet when the Cosmic Christ appears with his legions to assist these poor children of Helios and Vesta to restore the imagination of the very heart and the mind and the very brain itself, which has been tampered with by the taking in of drugs, then they declare that this is not lawful.

Gaze upon Beautiful Thoughtforms

Beloved ones, we do come. We come with a great gift. We see how even the very beating of the rock music upon these delicate membranes of your being has caused you to be a little less and a little less receptive to the delicate sendings of the Cosmic Christ to your soul.

And so we come with beauty, we come with nourishment, we come with thoughtforms, and we come with the statues that we have brought to our altar through many of your own hands so that you may gaze upon these archetypes of your internal reality.

---

*The phrase "it's just not cricket" is an English idiom that means something is unfair or dishonest. It is derived from the sport of cricket, which is regarded as a gentleman's game where fair play is paramount.

And in gazing upon them, you transfer to millions and millions of cells the image of the Buddha.

Do you know the transformation of consciousness that occurred even this morning through this ritual of going over and over again the images of the Buddha and the Mother?[8] Why, in each and every one of you there is now established that polarity, that figure-eight flow. And this is written in your etheric body and even in your physical cells so that when you take in nourishment and food and air and sunshine, the nutrients of life coming into your temple now flow after that basic matrix.

This is programming, not by rote but by the conscious cooperation of your soul with your Christ mind. Likewise, when you decree the same word several times, many times, you are making a deeper and deeper impression in your four lower bodies of living letters of sacred fire, impressing upon your being the worded mantras of the ascended masters.

And while, then, you are engaged in daily duties and other affairs, there is the natural breathing in and out of the Holy Spirit that passes through these beautiful matrices that you have lovingly, consciously, freely deposited in your superconscious, waking conscious, and subconscious mind. And so because energy flows through you as a giant Niagara Falls twenty-four hours a day because you have created so many, many of these perfect thoughtforms, we can release to you that great light that passes through you and then blesses the earth with the very fragrance that emits from these inner designs.

Many of the recordings that are made upon your bodies through the decrees are microscopic in size, and yet they fulfill the function of transmitting God's light and energy and of holding the balance for the earth. This is why we have recommended that mothers with child not look upon the television set or take in the substance of the media or partake of discordant art forms.

This is because during the period of gestation there is within the mother the multiplication of her ability to take in and pass on to the forming child the light-energy-consciousness that is around her. This ability, as all abilities and talents, is not one of discrimination. The talent is given. The individual by free will must discriminate in its use. And therefore the mother becomes a giant receiving station for the sendings of the Elohim and the archangels.

Now you see that the fallen ones have determined that mothers will not spend even five minutes in meditation daily, or even throughout the period of their pregnancy. And by creating all manner and manifestation of outer forcefields, these fallen ones have diverted the mother's attention and therefore they have succeeded in using this most amazing forcefield of the computer of the mind of God to transfer to the incoming child not the harmony of inner spheres but all of the degradation of outer spheres.

And thus these little children are born—born more and more a part of the degeneration spiral of the earth and her evolutions, which we are witnessing today.

A Counterfeit Path

The fallen ones who move among the children of God upon earth have taken their training from the archdeceivers of mankind at inner levels. Just as your souls journey to the retreats of the Great White Brotherhood, those who are committed to the path of ambition and pride journey to other "retreats" that are on the astral plane,[9] and there they meet individuals who pose as the most advanced adepts on the Path and are truly convinced at inner levels that they are working with the elite of earth's evolutions who are descended even from Almighty God himself. The false hierarchy has an entire evolution, all the way back to the one who sits on the throne, the counterfeit throne of God, the impostor of the Almighty One.

The souls who are duped are the souls who have not the sincere and pure desire for reunion with God. Nevertheless, they seem sincere in their activities. And those who train them give them to understand, by a very distorted means, what the goals of life are upon earth and how they [the trainers] are concerned for the greatest good and the greatest happiness and the greatest expansion for earth's people.

When you consider this, you must be aware of the fact that there is a danger among spiritual groups and religious teachings that those individuals who have not let go of or transmuted the desire for ambition—the desire for success through pride—will come into the circle of devotees, and by imitation they will present a counterfeit path, a counterfeit initiation, a counterfeit manifestation whereby the soul leaves the body temple and enters into the "etheric octave."

And so there have been movements that have, in actuality, promised soul travel to their devotees. There has been an invention of names of masters and contacts on earth galore. Many books and many organizations in North and South America, in Europe, and even in Africa have purported to represent the Brotherhood of light.

Beloved ones, you can see that the false hierarchy behind them is complete—that by their misuse of the energy of the chakras they too may create the simulation of vibration and all of that which appears to be real but is not. Now, when children of the light do not have a direct experience with the Holy Spirit, with the Lord Christ, with their own I AM Presence because they have placed other gods before them, they therefore do not have that level of discrimination.

Let the children of the light come, then, and sit at the feet of the ascended masters. Let them set aside all goals of self-aggrandizement—those very subtle desires whereby those on the psychic path or the so-called spiritual path see themselves as being above others and therefore able to command respect by their so-called powers. These powers range all the way from phenomena to actual healings to even that which appears to be the raising of the dead. This has been done by the fallen ones by mechanical means and even by the misuse of the energies of the chakras.

The Initiation of Finding Your Way Back to Me

Beloved ones, some of you have no idea the Path that you walk, the Path that you shall walk when you determine to become a disciple of the Cosmic Christ.

I come before you with utter love. It is not to shock or to frighten you but to tell you that when you plead with me from your heart for initiation, that initiation must first be your encounter with the one who is my counterfeit. For by law I must determine if you are worthy to stand in the presence of your own Christ Self and that level of scintillating light and cosmic consciousness that the LORD God has given to me.

These counterfeits are numerous, and so I say to you that initiation is not the mere touching of your chakras or the passing of a current of energy. It is sending you forth as though blindfolded and it is saying, "Now, find your way back to me *by vibration.* Meditate until you feel my presence as a pulsating, cosmic love-wisdom, and then direct your course to me, though you see me not."

And I can guarantee you that that course will then be fraught with those who will take you this way and that way into primrose paths, justified on the basis that they are constructive, they serve some human good, they serve some lesser purpose.

Therefore you say, "Why not combine them with the search for Maitreya, inasmuch as Maitreya is so far away and it is unlikely that I will find him today or tomorrow or the next? I will engage myself in this or that." And so you become entangled in the marshes, the lowlands, the deepest valleys, and even the sublevels of the earth, in the canyons of the astral plane, thinking you do God service.

The Mantle of Responsibility

I come, then, on the wake of the wave of light released in the dictations that have been given by our Brotherhood from this platform—dispensations of the thrust for purity and wisdom and love, dispensations whereby the teaching has gone forth on the mantle of responsibility.

Inasmuch as Alpha and Omega have communicated to you through the beloved God of Freedom their simple word, we are counting upon this body of lightbearers to secure the future of freedom on earth.[10]

I AM come. I come because I know well that for the accomplishment of the task in Saint Germain's name, in the name of the innocent souls of the innocent victims, you must have that Cosmic Christ initiation.

I also say to you that if you did not need the messenger, the messenger would not be here. It is quite simply a fact understood by the Brotherhood that you have many hurdles to jump before you have the full Christ-discrimination that will enable you to understand the difference between a bearer of light and one who is of the seed of the wicked.

Therefore, bypass not the counsel of the messenger, and do not fancy that in merely writing to us letters and communications and burning them, you will have the full manifestation in this octave of the deliberations of the Christ mind through the messenger.

It is well, then, for you to understand that we are the same being and consciousness, level upon level upon level, even as you see those mandalas of the Buddhas as they come in every level of cosmic consciousness.

So, then, as I AM in Spirit, so I AM in Matter. And therefore if you would have my counsel in Matter, and if the problem is pressing, and if it is a matter concerning life and death and the path of your soul and decisions you must make, do not allow the demons to tell you, "Mother is too busy. She will not hear from me. She will not read my letters. She does not have time to answer me."[11]

Beloved ones, this only necessitates a very large circumventing of the return and the answer to your request. For then by and by we must create the circumstances whereby the messenger comes to you, many times regretfully after it is too late and you have made decisions that have taken you far afield from the concentrated initiations of your life.

And of course, then, there are those chelas who fill their houses with focuses and photographs because these enable them to enter into a fanciful relationship with our Brotherhood. For you know, as we have said, pictures do not talk back, and so then you may imagine any response you desire from the ascended masters.

Well, beloved ones, our embodied Guru is one who talks back to you, and you must have the courage to hear that Word else dwell forevermore in that twilight area of the coward, fearing and trembling yet never knowing what in actuality is the Word of the LORD unto your soul.

Well, this is a decision that must be made, and a number have made it—the decision whether to be a part of the circle of our community, whether to be tied to one who will talk back to you and decipher for you the levels of your consciousness, or whether to be outside of the circle, to read the books, to take the teachings, do what you will with them, and chart for yourself a zigzag course.

Chart Your Course with Me

If you could only see yourselves in perspective—you who have desired to become a law unto yourself, with your ship at sea! I would like to show you where you have gone without the polestar, without the real and genuine tie. The zigzagging of your course has led you nowhere, even as the children of Israel wandered in that wilderness forty years when it would have required not even the fullness of a year to pass through.

All of this was because of their rejection of the Guru in embodiment. And the rejection of the Guru came because of the manifestation of discord, bickering, complaining, lamenting, always wanting something more, something better, never being satisfied—no, not with the daily manna that fell from the heavens as the mighty teaching of God, as nourishment for the soul, as food for the body; no, not being content with the miracles, the parting of the Red Sea, the writing of the tablets of the Law, the confounding of the Egyptians, and all that transpired even before the court of Pharaoh.

Was this enough? Nay, I tell you! For the rebellious ones it was not enough. And they continued to complain and to complain and to complain, and so they charted what might be considered, looking from our view, an amusing course.

One day you will sit with me, as I am the captain of a mighty ship, a sailing vessel in which I take you on journeys of the soul. And I will show you our charts and many layers of charts, and then you will be shown by me your own charting of your own course without the intercession of our Brotherhood.

And you will be amazed, beloved ones, to look at the track

of your life for many, many incarnations. Some of you, believe it or not, have never even left port. You have zigzagged back and forth within a few knots' distance, and yet it has taken perhaps thousands of years. But somehow, in the smallness and the smugness of the human mind, you have stood proudly at the helm of your vessel, considering that you were traversing miles and miles of a journey so utterly important unto the destiny of the planetary evolution.

We have seen enough of our Walter Mittys* on the Path. We have seen the deluded ones filled with fantasy. We have seen the more malicious, who have determined at all costs to control the messenger, to seize the light, but never to bend the knee before the law of love and the Path that is for their own way [of overcoming]. It is always tragic.

The Compromise of the Soul

But beloved ones, there is a certain sickness, a certain insanity, a certain condition of psychology that I would point out to those of you serving as counselors and ministers. It is that of individuals who have compromised their souls, and there is somehow a blind spot within them whereby they never truly understand that there comes an hour when because of the denial of Christ they are cut off from the access of the energy of our Brotherhood through the messenger because they have rejected the path of initiation. And they remain deluded with their quotations of scripture that the mercy of God endures forever.[12]

And so without the discipline of the law of the Christ, this disease cannot be cured because it demands a shock that is the very jogging of the cells of the brain and of the body, the shocking of those cells from their rebellious patterns and the bringing of

---

*Walter Mitty: a person who seeks escape from reality through daydreaming. The name is taken from the short story by James Thurber, "The Secret Life of Walter Mitty."

those cells back into alignment with the will of God. And because the minds of these individuals are crazed and full of self-pity and a sense of injustice, these individuals become angry and intensely malicious when they may no longer drink freely of the milk from the breast of the Mother.

Beloved ones, we must cut off the flow of light by the very mercy of the Law so that these individuals will no longer misqualify the great quantities of light that are available to the chelas who are tied to the chain of hierarchy. This is the mercy of the Law, but that mercy is rejected by the fallen ones. They have another mercy, and their mercy is called sympathy.

Sympathy with themselves makes them fail to see that the compassion of God acts in the defense of the soul against this wretched carnal mindedness that breeds disease. And that disease, known as the cancer of the soul and of the astral body, can and does spread among the children of God by the example of these fallen ones, who then—by their revenge and their resentment—move in echelons, especially in the entertainment industry, so that they may parade themselves before the children of God and again, by the flow of the attention, usurp their light.

As the children of God give these fallen ones their attention, over the return flow comes the out-of-rhythm cycles of the fallen ones' rebellion, comes their own self-pity, comes a lifestyle that is incompatible with a Christed one. And all of this feeds subconsciously into the souls of the lightbearers while they are having an evening of enjoyment and applauding their favorite stars. And so they surely become those stars, even as surely as you can become the Buddha and the Mother by equal if not less attention spans.

This quality and ability known as the plasticity of the soul and the being itself, the ability to take on and assimilate the object of one's affection, is the very means whereby God becomes God within you.

We cannot—we dare not—cut off this talent, this ability. For you see, though it might protect this generation from the fallen ones, it would also successfully exclude this generation from the light emanations of our offering, our humble offering of the spoken and the written Word and the teaching of the New Age.[13]

Now you see, beloved ones, how the poor and the needy and the fatherless must be fed and cared for by you, not simply by social welfare programs but by the much greater need for the programming of all society to the reflection of the blueprints of the etheric cities.[14] These souls must be protected by setting up forcefields of prayer and of the energies of Archangel Michael and by the perpetual prayer invoked by you for the protection of their chakras and their souls.

Beware of the Death Wish

When there is the vibration of the seed of the wicked, which contains within itself the desire for self-annihilation—the death wish, in psychological terms—that desire momentum is transmitted to all who are a part of an interchange with that individual. Beware, then, of those who have that death wish, that inverted desire that becomes the desire for self-annihilation.

Beloved ones, you all understand the meaning of the self to include every self of God. That meaning is also contained in the energy that is within the seed of the wicked. Therefore, listen well as I explain that the desire for self-annihilation is not fulfilled within the wicked but it is fulfilled by the destruction of other selves.

Therefore the death wish is transferred. And because in the death process there is the release of the energy of life from the matrix, as when a flower dies and the light goes back to God, so whenever there is the death of a soul of light there is a release of a tremendous amount of energy.

And so this desire for self-annihilation, the death wish, is always projected upon those who have the greatest light. For when they die, the one containing the death wish will assimilate that energy to perpetuate that same death desire. This is the insanity of insane minds. All who have betrayed the Lord Christ are considered insane and having the communicable illness of rebellion. Therefore we send our legions for the protection of the Christ consciousness upon earth.

When there is a soul or a body in the process of dissolution, decay, and death, and when that individual has been a part of the light in some form in this or previous incarnations, then during the period of the degeneration spiral there is a great deal of light that is being released from those cells, from that body temple. That light would flow naturally back to the Great Central Sun if it were not for the fact that those who are a part of these death cycles take that energy and use it over and over again. It should be compared to, beloved ones, the partaking of the very sewer of life and passing it through the body many times over.

The Cult of Sweet Death—
the Degenerate and Immoral

When energy passes through a body or passes through the chakras (because it passes through something that is not moving), there is a sensation of the friction between the movement of energy and the chakra or the vehicle that remains still. This release of energy as sensation is used for the heightening of sexual experience, of the pleasure cult, of drug experiences, and all forms of those hallucinations that come from the unreal world.

Let me state this again—that when there is the death of souls of light because they have rebelled against God, because they have been corrupted by rebellion, the process of decay, by its very definition, is a process of the release of energy. The energy released is itself misqualified energy. This energy, then, is regurgitated and re-assimilated as it passes through many times.

As the energy is passing through, it then may take on the simulation of life and its many processes. Therefore there is an entire evolution upon the planetary body who are a part of the spirals of death in this very hour, and these individuals are having a heyday of enjoyment. They seem to experience life intensely and richly, and they are motivated by intense sexual desire and the need for sensual experience. This is because they are in the very process of losing the soul's sensitivities and the contact with life, and so to keep that grasp on life they must create and re-create day by day those activities that are degenerate and immoral.

This, beloved ones, becomes the cult of death—the cult of sweet death whereby individuals enjoy the very last dregs of misqualified energy unto the hour of the death of the bodies* and the death of the soul.

Now, when children of the light who are daily giving all of their energy to God in service, in joy, in singing, and in all of the things that are a part of reality—when they come and observe the fun and the games and the activities of those individuals who are already in unreality, and if they are not taught by their parents to understand what is happening, they will be allured into these parties, into the taking of drugs, into the taking in of alcohol and massive amounts of sugar and unreal chemical foods.

And so the children of light go the way of a death generation simply because fathers and mothers do not have the courage to extend the discipline that may make them indeed unpopular with their own offspring but that will incur to them forever and forever the gratitude

---

*This may be referring to the four lower bodies (the etheric, mental, emotional, and physical bodies).

of the souls of their children, who after maturity will realize that they have been spared from the very deceptions of this age.

The Opening of the Way Is at Hand

I encourage you, then, to meditate deeply upon the great sphere of my cosmic consciousness, to penetrate the deeper mysteries of life and to not be satisfied with surface appearances. Beneath the surface, beloved ones, there are causes behind effects and other effects, and causes behind these, and they are almost a chain of causation and the effecting of cause that is a karmic chain that moves through the entire mass consciousness.

Motives must be studied—*not the smiles but the motives.* Discern motivation by the light of purity and then come to understand how you may well defend millions of souls in this age who would, if left alone and not tampered with, go straight to the throne of the Cosmic Christ. I am waiting to receive them, beloved ones. Go and find them. Take them by the hand and bring them to my fount of everlasting life.

In the name of the Father, the Son, and the Holy Spirit, I open the way of initiation for *all* who make known to me in this hour that they are desirous of this path even in the face of the information that I have given to you.

The opening of the Way is at hand. Let the wary, the courageous, and the soul filled with love fear not to step upon the threshold and to pass through from glory unto glory.

Amen.

July 2, 1978
Pasadena, California

*I say it unto you as it has been said in
all previous civilizations of planetary systems—
those who would bring an evolution
into a golden age must bring their
individual consciousness unto
the golden age of the
crown chakra.*

CHAPTER 6

The Initiation of the Law of the One in the Guru-Chela Relationship

If the world hate you, ye know that it hated me before it hated you.
If ye were of the world, the world would love his own: but because ye are not of the world, but I have chosen you out of the world, therefore the world hateth you.
Remember the word that I said unto you, The servant is not greater than his lord. If they have persecuted me, they will also persecute you; if they have kept my saying, they will keep yours also.
But all these things will they do unto you for my name's sake, because they know not him that sent me.
If I had not come and spoken unto them, they had not had sin: but now they have no cloak for their sin.
He that hateth me hateth my Father also.
If I had not done among them the works which none other man did, they had not had sin: but now have they both seen and hated both me and my Father.
But this cometh to pass, that the word might be fulfilled that is written in their law, They hated me without a cause.

~ John 15:18–25

Hail, O initiates of Maitreya! Hail, O legions of the flame! I come in the great light of illumination and the great frequency of the wisdom of the mind of God. I come, entering now into the great consciousness of the peoples of the earth. I come in the flaming Presence of the Lord God.

I come now into the crown chakras of the children of the Sun. I come to initiate you out of the light of your own inner attainment. For if ye are the salt of the earth, and ye are, then that salt is the measure of light and of attainment. And if the salt has lost its savor,[1] then I say, you have lost the light of your attainment and it remains latent within the Great Causal Body of the universe, the collective awareness of the universal Christ, but you yourself are without access to it.

Now you may understand how the salt may have lost its savor. It is when you have in past ages, over the millennia, garnered unto yourselves great light, and then you became satisfied, in a quiescent state in the earth, and therefore a perversion of the great light of the Buddha.

For the Buddha is not sleeping. The Buddha is in the active rest of the wholeness of Alpha and Omega whereby the whirling consciousness of the mind of God is ever present, keeping the vigil of the flame of life on earth and in heaven. And some have come, then, to an idolatry in the schools of Buddhism. And you, my chelas who come to be taught of Maitreya, must come first and foremost to know that the great realization of the mind of God must be an active peace.

And that active peace is the peace of the sword. And therefore the peace of the sword is the sacred Word, but the sacred Word must first be spoken in the heart. Thus, there is an outer stillness and an outer silence while the soul goes within into the secret chamber of the heart, there to commune with a Buddha, there to commune with Maitreya, there to know the Word because the Word is first whispered as the soundless sound within the ear.

And then it echoes within the vastness of consciousness, and then it becomes that firing within of the Great Spirit. Then when the hour for the soul is come to manifest thy kingdom on earth as it is in heaven, then the spoken Word in the earth becomes the great power to implement peace.

Our Dedication of This Planetary Sphere Is unto the Guru-Chela Relationship

I AM Maitreya. I stand in the Great Hall of China. I stand now within the Senate of the United States of America. I stand in the Oval Office. I stand in the offices of the heads of state of all nations. I AM the initiator of the souls of earth and of her evolutions and I say to you: Our dedication of this planetary sphere is unto the Guru-chela relationship,[2] which comes now in this age with the coming light of the Buddha and of the Mother, with the coming of the great Gurus, the ascended masters, and their embodied representative.

I issue the judgment of the Lord Jesus Christ unto the nations, for the hour of the judgment is come.[3] And as it pertains to the light of the path of initiation, so it is spoken by the LORD God that those who would save the earth, those who would rule in the footstool kingdom, must come now and bend the knee before the hierarch of the Aquarian age, the ascended master Saint Germain, confessing that the Lord Christ is indeed come in the flesh within him and within his embodied messenger.

Therefore, because that incarnation of the Word is intact on Terra, there is hope. There is opportunity. And every chela of the Word incarnate is a follower of the Lamb, and every chela that is a part of the great body and mind and soul and heart of that Lamb therefore receives the sponsorship of the Four and Twenty Elders[4] for the implementation of the ten-year plan of the Buddha and the plan of the age.[5]

Souls Must Learn to Raise Up the Mother Light

My beloved, I bring to you the great burden of light, accelerating now as the mighty golden-white sphere of initiation. The hour of the judgment is come, and the judgment is the hour of initiation.

Therefore I say to you, as I said in Eden unto the twin flames appointed by God to be an example of the Path—I say to you as I spoke it again in the inner retreats of Atlantis, in the vastness of the Himalayan caves; I say it unto you as it has been said in all previous civilizations of planetary systems—*those who would bring an evolution into a golden age must bring their individual consciousness unto the golden age of the crown chakra.*

They must then learn to raise up the Mother light and to know that unless the heart is set aright with the heart of the Cosmic Christ and the one whom he has anointed as the hierarch of the two-thousand-year cycle, then that one cannot have the all-power of God to move the mountains of adversity, to challenge the fallen ones, and to set to deliverance the captives—the captives of maya, the captives of duality.

The Law of *One*

Our religion is a Law of the One. It is the Law of *One*. And the religion of two or more is a religion of idolatry. Let there be no idolatry here! Let only the oneness of God as the single Person of God in the fullness of the Trinity within you be that Reality! My beloved, whenever there are two, there is then idolatry.

Ponder upon this great mystery of the Holy Grail, for the very nature of a mystery is that it may be spoken on the one arm of the cross and then upon the other arm of the cross. And the dividing of the way of Alpha and Omega is the perception, the resolution of the truth of the great mystery within the center of the cosmic cross of white fire.

This is how you arrive at the dissertations of the Buddhas and of the teachings. For out of the statement of Alpha and Omega, out of the right and the left, the resolution of truth is come. Out of the One, the many; yet the many are the One. Therefore, perceive the One in the many.

Perceive the one light of the entire Spirit of the Great White Brotherhood. Perceive the Holy Spirit in every ascended master, yet one Spirit. Perceive the Son in every son of God, yet one Son. Perceive the Father infinitely manifest in every electron as a law of universal energy, yet always one Father, Son, Holy Spirit but only one expression of the One.

Understand the science. For the simple perception of this science and this mystery of the Cosmic Christ—its contemplation even for a moment—will be the healing and the alignment of worlds beyond worlds.

And therefore the cosmic consciousness of the law of God, endowed by wisdom and by love, is the liberation of your soul. It is not the repetition of these words as an intellectual concept but it is entering into the Word itself as the energy of a cosmos. Feel the quivering of that creation in the Creator and know not a duality but a oneness.

Oneness Consumes Idolatry

I AM that being within you, but you have not known me as yourself and therefore you perceive me as speaking unto you.

But when you see me as I AM, you will see yourself as I AM and then you will know the Law of the One.

This is why I have come from out the great, Great Central Sun to teach at Summit University.[6] It is because the Guru-chela relationship is intact and I cannot be except where there is that flow from hierarchy unto hierarchy, as a great chain upon the Christmas tree.

Link by link, the adornment of the Tree of Life is a rising caduceus composed of each individual's own caduceus, and there is one singular caduceus universally in the cosmos. And if ye would be of that one, then drink of my cup. Drink ye all of it.[7] For I AM the same, the One, the universal Christ individualized in Krishna, in Lord Jesus.

Let all argumentation cease. For each son of God is supreme and absolute unto himself when that son of God is the light emanation of God. Are there a million billion sunbeams, or but one?

Almighty God, now thy oneness, let it be within these halls where I stand. For oneness itself is the judgment of all idolatry. Oneness itself consumes all unlike itself.

Do Not Cross the Line to Become the Guru When You Are the Chela

I come, then, for the transfer of this cosmic consciousness. And do not wonder or do not question why or how the disciplines come to you who are privileged to know myself in this flesh.*

Do not then cross the line to become the Guru when you are the chela, but understand that the Guru will no longer explain why this intact circle of lightbearers must be the holding of a great chalice of light unto the earth.

It is the word of the Lords of Karma[8] unto you that if this nation under God is to be saved, it will be saved only by those

---
*in this messenger

who have the contact under God of Saint Germain, of the Cosmic Christ, of every ascended master who is one and in and a part of every other ascended master. For we are one and we will not be divided by any mechanization of religion or manipulation of the souls of the people into compartments of consciousness.

We are one. Our message is one. Our messenger is one. And that victory is your own. And therefore we look to these, and these alone, to occupy the positions in the economy and in the government and in education, who will set the policy of the Great White Brotherhood in the physical plane.

A Message from God the Father

Beloved ones, I come to you with the truth spoken by Almighty God this day, God the Father, who has said unto me:

> Maitreya, go forth and mediate on behalf of these souls, and tell them that there are many well-meaning souls on earth who have seen a portion of the truth, but the fallen ones have amassed their anti-power, anti-wisdom, anti-love.
>
> They have imitated the disciplines of Serapis Bey. They have imitated the culture of Paul the Venetian. They have imitated the science of Hilarion. They have imitated the ritual and the transmutation and the freedom of Saint Germain. They have imitated the God-government of El Morya. They have imitated the wisdom of the sages Lanto and Confucius. They have imitated the purity of the Mother. They have imitated the way of service of Nada. [These are the seven chohans of the rays.][9]
>
> They have set up their welfare systems as an imitation of the path of Christ unto that service. They have set up their

priesthood in imitation of the priesthood of Melchizedek.[10] They have imitated all things. They have organized. They have put together vast powers and wealth to sustain their imitation of cosmic abundance and supply.

In every area of the manifold works of my seven sons, these chohans of the rays, the fallen ones have attempted and they have indeed created their counterfeit society.

And therefore go forth, Maitreya, and tell the souls of light that if they are to succeed in overthrowing all of this pollution of the light of Omega, all of this pollution in the Matter sphere, all of this perversion of the Mater-realization, then they must have the all-power of the Father, of the Son, and of the Holy Ghost dwelling within them—and the all-wisdom and the all-love. For only Reality, the Reality of God, can overthrow the counterfeit.

And therefore, take note that those who see the error of the fallen ones and who speak of it, who isolate it, who point it out—and yet have not the path of initiation under the Gurus of the age—will not have the power to enter into the temple, into the Great Hall of China, into the Senate, into the House of Representatives, into the offices of the presidents of the nations to challenge the fallen ones and their amalgamation of power and their reasoning and their rationale.

And therefore, speak unto them, Maitreya! Speak as I have spoken! For the Lord God has need of one thing, and that is the true and faithful disciples of Christ who will endure all things unto the end. And by enduring hatred and persecution, they are then become the fiery vortex of myself.

As I abide in the Central Sun, I will abide within their

hearts as that all-consuming fire. And only those who have the tie to the chain of being will sustain, will withstand, will turn back, will withhold, and will be on the line of the sacred fire.

And then, O my son, give to them my comfort! For they will feel desolate in the awareness of the handful of chelas who are truly the chelas of the Great White Brotherhood upon earth!

Tell them of the Holy Spirit and of the comfort flame! Tell them that they must go forth and cut free souls of light whom I have planted as seed in the earth—good seed, seed that will respond, seed that will understand by great enlightenment, by the great Word of the Cosmic Christ that I have placed within you, my son Maitreya.

God Will Invest the All-Power of Heaven and Earth within the Chela

I have come forth in that great highlight of the mind of Alpha. I have come forth in the purity of Omega given unto me. And that purity that I hold in my cup is sufficient, O my chelas, *to wash, to wash, to wash* the Mater body of the earth, to cleanse it of the foul and unclean spirits that have invaded the domain of the chohans of the seven rays.

I call you, souls of light! This is the cycle of the turning. This is the moment, the turning point of life when God will invest the all-power of heaven and earth within the chela who espouses the will of God and who understands that the one who will save the earth is the one God—that no outer person, outer mind, outer self, no matter what the human qualifications, can bring to bear upon the world today even one movement, one turning of energy without that presence of light and the vast chain that is ensouled by every ascended master, archangel, angel, and cosmic being. You are a part of all of this power when you walk in the name of the Lord, and none of this is unto you if you cannot confess that he is come in the flesh.

Study the mysteries of the Word incarnate. Study the mysteries of the Holy Grail.[11] Be willing, then, to be that manifestation. For the hour is coming when souls of light must recognize that in the night, in the light, in the Omega, in the Alpha, there is a keeping of the vigil, there is a keeping of the flame.

In the Matter sphere our messenger keeps the flame of light as a spiritual teaching, as the exposure, as the unveiling of Good and Evil. And all chelas of Maitreya, of Saint Germain and of the chohans, have the obligation to translate that vigil from the Spirit sphere of Matter into the Matter sphere of Matter—thence to go forth from Camelot,[12] north, south, east, and west.

The Extension of Chelaship unto the Nations Is the Only Hope

Beloved ones, Alpha has told me—*Alpha has told me that it is the extension of chelaship unto the nations that is the only hope for those nations that would be free.* This is your challenge! This must be your pursuit—to present the vigil of the flame of the sacred fire and to translate it unto the evolutions of earth in your chosen field!

Beloved ones, you have heard of this teaching. Hear it now as the formal announcement of the Cosmic Christ: If you would be the instrument of the salvation of the earth, you cannot have merely a smattering of the teaching and a few decrees and then hurry about in the business world imagining that you do God service. You must come for the empowering of your flame and of your temple. You must rearrange yourself and be inconvenienced if you would have the power of God.

Therefore does Alpha say: "*Cease* to look without this company for saviours in the economy or in the government or in education or in science or in the entire system of welfare and the community! *Cease* to look to those who say the right words, who are the good people of the earth but who do not have the tie to the all-power of God through the chain of the great Gurus of the age!"

Beloved ones, you must understand that the good people of the earth have been crying out in outrage against the seed of the wicked, even though they have not known that seed for hundreds of thousands of years! The same ones who have spoken to you—wonderful souls[13]—have sounded a warning. But those who have conquered have been those who have been willing to become the Christ by the path of initiation.

And therefore if you wait for saviours who have not come in the name of the Lord Saint Germain, Jesus Christ, Mother Mary, Gautama Buddha, with the exclusion of none, you will then be waiting for a salvation that will not come!

God! God! God in You Is the Key!

And so I say, in the name of my father Gautama, *Awake! Awake!* Cease the idolatry that looks without, that looks outside of yourself! For there is the sleep—*there is the sleep* of meditation, imitating the great statues of the Buddha while not knowing of a cosmos inside of that statue, inside of that one Lord of the World[14] that is teeming with life in action, that is cosmic consciousness, that is God-government, that is all that is required.

O beloved, *God! God! God in you is the key!* Now cease to look to God in another, for you cannot control the free will of another. You can never be dependent upon the actions of another from moment unto moment, but you can depend upon God. And the God incarnate who is most dependable is the God who has become the chela, and the chela who has become the God by the Law of the One and who has rested his life upon the trust of the messenger—the Guru beyond the Guru—and therefore has the open flow of a fountain of life.

Trust is the beginning of the Path!
Trust is the beginning of the Path!
Trust is the beginning of the Path!

And this nation of "In God We Trust" is a nation that can only survive under the great Gurus, the ascended masters. Learn the lesson well. Come to be tutored by the Guru Mother. Come, then, to receive an understanding of what must be added unto the initiations of your soul as preparation in the universities of the Spirit[15] and the universities of the world.

Understand that as the extension of God—complete and whole in love—you will overcome. And unless you become that extension, then the mere words, the mere repetition, the mere giving of books will not be the salvation.

Beloved ones, God has decided to save the earth through his instrument. *You* are that instrument! I AM that instrument! And you cannot account for any other instrument save the one that is the cross of white fire where you are. I press upon you now the ultimate sense of responsibility to be God in the highest order, in the highest sense of the word.

Beloved ones, I cherish the souls of light who have gone forth nation to nation, not knowing that they have gone in my name and yet giving the purity of the message. Let us pray unto our Father that at inner levels they shall be united and they shall have the whole armour of the teaching and the sword of the right use of the I AM THAT I AM.

Let us pray that those children of God will swiftly elect to be made Sons of God by belief on the name of the Lord Jesus Christ and in the inevitability of the incarnate Word in themselves. He is the power to make of you Sons of God,[16] which means *Christs of God*, *the* Christ incarnate.

Beloved ones, not one individual who is without that awareness, whether to the right or to the left of the human consciousness, has the power to sustain a flame that will consume darkness.

The Purpose of the Incarnate Word

Let us speak, then, for a moment, of the understanding of those scriptures spoken to you.[17] They are not the oft-repeated scriptures. They are repeated only by the initiates. The understanding of human hatred of the Christ can only be understood by the one who is standing in the seat of authority, who stands in that position of light. The one who is in that great threefold flame then knows the vibration of the hatred that comes upon those who would be Christs and are Christs.

This hatred, then, is all anti-God manifestation in Matter, all perversion of Mother and within Mother, all of the elements of the consciousness of God—Father, Son, Holy Spirit, and Mother. Understand, then, that when the Lord Christ and I promise to you persecution, we promise to deliver to you the momentum of planetary karma that must pass into the flame where God is.

And God is where the Guru is. God is where the chela is. And in all other people he remains dormant in the Great Causal Body and sealed as a flickering candle upon the heart, with only a sufficient light to sustain the propagation of the individual race of mankind.

Understand, then, that that persecution comes with all of its intensity *only where God is!* And inasmuch as persecution cannot pass into the great planes of Spirit, into the great throne room of Alpha and Omega, it comes, then, when Alpha and Omega embody within the Word incarnate, within the embodied Guru, and within the embodied chelas. Understand this great mystery—that this is where God then becomes vulnerable, and God must make *himself* vulnerable.

He must give opportunity to all evolutions to express their free will toward him and yet without violating the great sphere of energy. Hence, the purpose of the incarnate Word is always for the judgment of those who have abused that Word. Cast out of heaven, then, they abide in the earth plane. They dwell there, and there is where the judgment shall be.

Ponder, then, the meaning of being God where you are. Ponder the understanding that only he who knows the Law of the One, that knows he is God, that knows he is God because he is a link in the chain of the Great White Brotherhood—only that one can stand before Pilate and be the truth even while Pilate questions "What is truth?"[18] because there is no truth within him. And therefore he himself is judged as the anti-God in the presence of God.

The Preparation of Our Chelas

We begin the most serious preparation of our chelas that has ever been attempted since the sinking of Atlantis. We begin an intensity and a discipline that is for those who understand that the age hangs in the balance—the balance of the decision of the individual chela.

We begin a discipline meet for the armies of the Faithful and True.[19] We will not withhold that intensity, and we will not stand for those in our midst who simper and whimper and complain of the intensity of the cause.

The fallen ones, who imitate the path of initiation, have their disciplined armies, have their disciplined students. And those who understand terrorism and the tactics of terror and agitation and propaganda and all of the cunning lies that they enter into the marts of ideas, become the excelling ones who excel in discipline. We will not have it! Serapis Bey has come to inaugurate a feast of light, planting a flame of purity and the love of discipline within you.

Now, if you would save the earth from the third cataclysm and America from the third vision,[20] understand that this is the hour to realize that all sacrifices that have gone before will come to naught unless your own sacrifices become the capstone in the great pyramid of the building of America and of Western civilization.

Let the indulgent ones *leave!* Let the halfhearted ones *leave!* Let those who pick apart and criticize and gossip concerning our messengers and our chelas *leave!* We are not interested in numbers. We are interested in the single-minded son of God who knows that God in him is sufficient unto the hour.

There are places for those who desire a softer way, diffused, where they do not see reality because they have not yet determined to put on their spectacles and leave them on and see what is light, what is darkness, and see the hummingbird and see the dove and see the spume of the salt of the sea.

This Is an Hour of Decision

I AM Maitreya. I come in a great sphere of light. I come because you have welcomed me. I come because you have made the trek to be a part of a circle of fire. And you who have come to warm yourselves, you have found it not so warm here at Camelot—and there is the point. For you must understand that the only fire that can warm you is the fire in your own heart, banked by love and virtue and service. O beloved ones, a few physical hardships teach the soul a multitude of truths.

And so my beloved, this is an hour of decision. You may have heard the teaching for many years. You may be lulled by the music and the voice of the teaching. But this is no ordinary communication. It is the pressing down upon you of the great mind of God and a realism with which many of the lightbearers have not been able to deal, even in recent months.

It is a realism conveyed to me by the Council of the Royal Teton, the Darjeeling Council, your messenger Lanello,* and all the way back to Alpha—a realism of the present amalgamation of forces and powers in the systems of these governments. The conspiracy is well on its way, beloved. It is directed against the soul of the individual who has determined to become God!

Now, then, we will see that no matter how great the mountain of darkness, that mountain can be leveled by the voice of *Elohim! Elohim! Elohim!* As the seven builders of form created form, so they can unbuild that form. They can withdraw the light of the form in an instant. So the energy locked into world conquest and world dominion can be withdrawn in a moment.

Why does God wait? He waits for God in the chela to be ready. For with the withdrawal of the power that has built the vain systems of the earth comes a collapse—a great collapse, a great cataclysm in the social order. And God desires that God shall survive in the earth in his people!

I warn you, then, of your dalliance, of allowing yourselves to be tied to systems that are internally self-destructive because they are built upon a foundation of hatred of the Guru, hatred of the Mother, hatred of Maitreya.

We Stand in Defense of Our Chelas

Do you wonder why I am the Buddha who has been coming? I have been coming and yet not manifest in the earth because of

---

*The messenger Mark L. Prophet made his ascension in 1973 and is now called the ascended master Lanello.

the hatred of me as the person of Maitreya since the expulsion of Adam and Eve from the Garden of Eden, since the judgment of Cain, since the judgment of the Serpent.

There is a resentment in the children of God of the Guru who has withdrawn his power and his light. And because there have now been some who have consumed [transmuted] that resentment and that ignorance of the Guru and his law, I have come. I have become that one in Matter as I have always been in Spirit.

Did you think that [I did not come because] it was a process of evolution and that Maitreya had not yet passed his initiations?

Well, my beloved, it is Maitreya in the chela! It is the chela who is becoming Maitreya who must pass the initiations that we long ago have passed and that we have held in the vastness of our cosmic consciousness.

Do not limit the coming of the Buddhas, and do not attempt to intellectualize their path. You do not know the vastness of our being, and therefore be content to ponder the vastness of your own. You do not know the vastness of the being of the twin flames of our messengers, and therefore be not concerned. For everyone who comes to earth must have a human vehicle, as you yourselves do have.

We will not allow the criticism of your human vehicle so long as you do not allow the criticism of our own. For we stand in defense of our chelas. Our chelas are ourself! There is no separation! There is no lesser love! There is no lesser consideration!

When you enter that path, you are one, and we do not judge by levels of karma but by levels of commitment. If your untransmuted karma be great, we behold your causal body. We behold present effort. We give total opportunity for the soul to prove herself today where she failed yesterday.

Can you do any less for those who represent us and who have been faithful year after year, aeon upon aeon? Therefore, do not question our judgment when we assign chelas a work in the Work of God.

Fear Not

We come. We see. We are the conquerors of human creation. We invite you to conquer with us. We show you how. We place in your hand not only a sword but a plow.

We show you how to plow a deep furrow in the human consciousness, how to plant the seed of the Cosmic Christ. We show you how to whirl that sling and slay the Goliaths of the age. They are many!

And with what tutoring did David come? He came with an anointing, and it was sufficient. He came with a light and a determination to bow before the LORD God and to serve him, and him alone.

Therefore I say, fear not. Do not think that Maitreya is unreasonable. Maitreya presents the truth. And you will go forth, for I ordain you, two by two. And you will bring in the souls who have the inner as well as the outer attainment to go straight to the top of the nations of the earth and to reverse the tide.

But you must be wide awake and aware and understand that our Saint Stephen of the hour will live and not die, will receive those stones and make of them tomes of wisdom to throw back to the Pharisees and Sadducees and to the people—wisdom to confound them.[21]

Make of those stones bread of life unto the multitudes. Make of those stones coals of fire flung into the very midst of those who are in their secret chambers plotting even now the death of the lightbearers. They have no power to destroy the Word, for the Word lives in you.

Make of those stones the hurling of the whirling centers of the seven chakras, and hurl those spheres of light as you stand in the great rainbow of the mighty Elohim and see how God in you will create and re-create an earth and her evolutions.

This is the opportunity. This is the option of the hour. The only one who can make certain the prophecy is *you!*

December 31, 1978
Camelot
Los Angeles County, California

*The momentum of the
violet light within you
is your ability to magnetize
that energy of transmutation.
A miracle, beloved ones,
is sudden transmutation.*

CHAPTER 7

The Garden of Eden

Removing the Splinters from the Soul

As the musical sounds of the devotions of India sound forth and fill the air with the vibration of the Word, I am come. I, Maitreya, receive the devotions of the pure in heart.

I receive the devotions, the very distillations of a soul's offering unto the Most High God. And I was there when Cain made his offering unto the Lord, when Abel made his offering unto the Lord, and the acceptability of the offering is in the purity of the devotion.[1]

This day many devotions rise as incense from the temples and the mosques, the churches and the sanctuaries of earth. As the incense bears the fragrance of its source, so the prayers of men and women and children bear the vibration, the very odor or the fragrance (as the case may be) of the motive of the heart in prayer.

Some pray to be thought well of men. Some pray that they might receive power and use it against one another. And some pray for the very union of the soul with God, that it might be a gift upon the altar of humanity for the salvation of the souls.

Some desire reunion simply to experience the bliss of reunion. Others see reunion as the means to the end—that end, that goal of life being the establishment once again of God consciousness upon the earth.

Thus, let mankind examine the motives of their own heart first, and let the Lord Christ come into the heart this day! Let the heart become the threshing floor and let there be a separation of the chaff and the wheat. Let the separation be so that the purification of the body of God might make a more perfect instrument.

The Intrusion of the Seed of the Wicked as Splinters in the Body of God

When mankind have examined their own heart's motives, when they have found there the flaws of inordinate desire and an actual attempt to use the light of God to cover their own sins, to cover their own darkness, let them pray that the LORD God will come and extract those splinters—splinters that are not of God but of the Satans who walked the earth,[2] the fallen ones who came as the Watchers of old to mingle their seed with the daughters of men and to thereby produce the offspring that were known as giants in those days[3]—giants, for they came forth out of the fallen power of fallen angels and united with that which was a mere mortality.

The attempt of Lucifer and the fallen ones to blend the seed of God with the seed of mortals and to thereby seize a light that they no longer had has produced a race of people upon the earth this day who must always and always come closer to the light in order to continue to cover themselves with a veil of light, whereas inwardly they are ravening wolves. Inwardly they rebelled against the law of God but they continually seek to hide their origin and their destiny.

Once again the ascended master Enoch walks through the highways of America. He walks midst the children of the light. He comes, "the seventh from Adam,"[4] the son of the mother and the father of the children of the light of Abraham.

Enoch stood in the Presence of God in the earth.[5] He had cosmic consciousness. He ascended through the planes of heaven, which registered as a great cosmic chord of cosmic consciousness within his own seven chakras of being. And therefore he was able to stand and to behold the visions of God, of heaven and earth and all that it contains, and of Light and Darkness and the challenge of the Light by that Darkness in that original rebellion.

And therefore he left a record for the sons and daughters of God concerning the intrusion of the seed of the wicked as splinters in the body of God and their attempt to intrude within the souls of lightbearers splinters that have become flaws in the diamond of the heart of our devotees.

We come to extract the splinters by the surgery of the Lord Jesus Christ, of the Cosmic Christ, of your own Christ Self—the surgery of the removing of those seeds of rebellion and disobedience and disorder and chaos, and even a challenging of the LORD God himself.

Let those, then, who with the fallen ones take their oaths and swear by the LORD God Almighty and by his name to destroy his children, let them know that in that hour of the denial of the flame of God, God so denies their own flame. Let those who walk in the imitation of the Watchers and the Satans know that they will so be judged with their seed. And let those who walk in the imitation of the Christed ones, the anointed ones, also know that they will be judged with the anointed ones.

Heed the Mighty Word of Enoch

Let the children of the light, whose soul light has been compromised, listen well. For the teaching of the great Teacher is nigh. And the ascended master Enoch comes to give to you the understanding of your own cosmogenesis, of your own history, of your own evolution of light, and of the battle of Armageddon that has been waged since the hour of the casting out of the fallen ones out of the heavens into the earth.[6]

See, then, that you heed the mighty word of Enoch and that you receive the impetus of the warning of the one who descended from Adam, who bore that mantle and who stands in the very midst of the children of God once again to summon them back to the highest mountain, back to the very places of light, back to that peak, that awareness, that oneness, that Mount Zion where the children of God were gathered and from whence some of the children of God descended to partake not of Christ's communion cup but to commune in the cups of the fallen ones and to drink with them the blood of the martyrs.[7]

These Splinters Shall Be Removed by the Great Gift of Miracles

I AM Maitreya. I come also with the mighty action of transmutation. For these splinters shall be removed by the gift of healing, by the great agency of healing, the Holy Ghost in the Lord Jesus Christ within you. And it shall come by the great gift of miracles, which signifies the hour of transmutation, the dissolving by the universal solvent—the violet transmuting flame itself—of those infiltrations and penetrations into the very auras of the lightbearers by the odor of the impure motive of the hearts of the seed of the fallen ones.

Let clarity and the crystal clarity of truth come forth. Let each soul of light who yearns for oneness realize that even as there has been an invasion of this solar system by those of evil intent from other systems of worlds, so there is an invasion of the body of earth, of the astral sheath of the earth, and even of your own temple—an invasion of those energies that are not your own and yet have remained with you for thousands of years, causing therefore great grief and the striving within your being against an adversary that you have not understood, whose face and name you have forgotten and yet whose face and name you once saw clearly.

The Separating of Light and Darkness within You

In the hour of confusion, in the hour of the intensification of illusion, it is the attempt of the fallen ones to confuse truth and error, light and darkness, and to create a blending to confute the Word of God and to confuse the little children.

Clearly it is the Word of God delivered unto the messengers of truth that once again is a mighty sword separating light and darkness within you so that you can recognize a healthy cell from a diseased cell and treat the one and invigorate the other.

Beloved ones, to give more energy to the diseased cell in some cases will cause the disease to grow, to increase. And therefore, often the withdrawal of the light from the diseased cell—which is diseased because it has been in rebellion against the light—is the great mercy of God on behalf of the healthy cell that must now have free and living, moving access unto the light of God, unhampered by the burdensome cells that encroach upon the flame of the living.

Thus it is the borning, the dying, the resurrection, the miracle of spring, the great miracle of Eastertide that is the new birth. And therefore with the coming of the new birth, certain cells within the consciousness pass through the degeneration spiral unto death, unto cancellation, unto annihilation. And that energy is recycled through the Great Central Sun so that the cell that is alive—because the threefold flame is the energy of that cell—can increase, can multiply, can propagate and create year upon year more beauty and more light and the greater fulfillment of the incarnate Word.

Elemental life is dedicated to the new birth in the floral offerings of spring, in the great green of the science of healing that you see emerging upon the hillsides.

Those Who Are of the Light Must Come Up Higher

O blessed ones of the sacred fire, when the great Gurus return to the scene of the activities of their chelas, there is an alchemy that must take place, there is a transmutation. And those who are of the light must come up higher; those who are not must realize their accountability for their darkness.

As Mother Mary said, "You cannot trifle with the Word"[8]— no, not with the message, no, not with the messenger of truth. And ye are all messengers of truth, even as the light of truth is the Christ Self within you.

Either we create a platform for truth, its accessibility, its acceptability, or we do not. But we do not create a platform where individuals may come in and challenge that Word as the very sacred fire that is the open fount of life flowing and nourishing the whole body of God, worlds without end. Therefore he who challenges one position in the order of hierarchy challenges all, even as he who breaks one point of the Law is guilty of breaking the whole law.[9]

Our Camelot is the Mystery School that opens the doors once again to the great challenges and the testings of the Garden of Eden, which was closed thousands upon thousands of years ago. The opening of these doors is the opening of the great inner temples of the Great White Brotherhood to souls of light upon earth. Never in all eternity has the Lord God allowed the great circle of Eden to be violated by the rebellious ones, and therefore he will not allow it in this age.

The keeping of the way of the Tree of Life is the assignment unto the messenger and the chelas of the ascended masters, making this activity unique among all others upon earth. Though many [other activities] have benign services and even some measure of our sponsorship, it is given to this one to open the way of the Mystery School, with its initiations, with its rigors, with its demands for an unquenchable love of God to be flowing in the heart.

That heart in you is the Sacred Heart of Jesus. It is the Immaculate Heart of Mary. As you meditate upon those hearts, think, then, upon this great truth—that every ascended master, every saint, every angel contains the mighty momentum of the sacred heart brimming with the very body and blood of Christ.

Why, in the very contemplation of that light, your souls might soar into *samadhi* if you would only but touch the essence of the Word that I give.

Miracles Are the Alchemy of the Violet Ray

I come to make plain the truth. I come to show you that if the gift of miracles delivered by the Holy Ghost were not necessary, it would not be given, it would not be ordained by God. Miracles are the alchemy of the violet ray of the seventh age. Miracles are the gift of Saint Germain.

The momentum of the violet light within you is your ability to magnetize that energy of transmutation. A miracle, beloved ones, is sudden transmutation. And sudden transmutation takes place because someone in the universe has garnered enough light, enough violet flame to inject such a momentum, such a portion of energy, that the action of that violet flame causes instantaneous change in the etheric plane, the mental plane, the emotional plane, and the physical plane. [See inset "The Sacred Gift of the Violet Flame," pp. 117–21.]

Therefore, to be the instrument of this great light you must have an equivalency of that light in your chakras and in your aura because, as you know, even the great miracle-healing drugs can produce death when too great a quantity is used. This is because there is not a corresponding balance within the body temple, and therefore that which is healthy in some doses becomes lethal in others. So it is true with the violet flame.

When you evoke the violet flame from God, you are the Omega polarity of that violet flame and you are given the Alpha polarity of that which you already contain. And when Alpha and Omega converge within you as the plus and the minus of the seventh ray, there is an acceleration so that with each invocation of the violet flame there is always the increase—the increase through your individual Christ consciousness. And that increase accrues to the momentum of the Omega energy that you are building in your chakras.

Therefore when you invoke the violet flame today, you receive the matched energy of Alpha. And when that matched energy descends and you meditate upon the great love of the seventh ray, there is a burst of energy that is the Cosmic Christ consciousness within you, and your Omega reserve increases.

So the next round of the evocation of the light of God produces another accelerated spiral, a greater momentum of the light of Alpha until you become a whirling sun center of violet flame, a central sun magnet verily whirling and attracting that momentum of violet flame that is in your own causal body of light.

Increase the Violet Flame That You Carry within Your Aura

Therefore, your first initiation in the violet flame is to be able to magnetize, to pull down from your causal body the great momentum of freedom that your soul has won through aeons and aeons of service to the Ancient of Days, who is the great carrier of the light of freedom unto the universes. And thus when you draw down your own momentum of the violet flame from your causal body, instantaneously you are then able to manifest the miracle of the Spirit body of your life, which in turn once again increases the violet flame that you carry within your aura.

And the goal of that exercise, you see, is to make you a balanced figure-eight flow so that ultimately the momentum of freedom of your causal body is in perpetual flow, perpetual motion over the figure-eight spiral. And then, you see, the great flow of that single band of the violet flame makes you a great carrier of the miracle of the Holy Ghost.

The miracle gift of healing from the Maha Chohan[10] gives to you, then, the award of being able to also draw down the great momentum of violet flame from the ascended masters' causal bodies, from the entire Spirit of the Great White Brotherhood, from Alpha and Omega, the very Selfhood of God.

The Seeds of Rebellion and Discontent

Understand, then, that as you come together, even in the cold and early hours of the morning, you are giving that application [to the violet flame] that is opening the way for your individual freedom and all that you desire to do for those who are sinful and sick and have diseased cells in the body of God.

The miracle of the violet flame is necessary for the dissolving of those energies that the fallen ones have attempted to insert within the solar system, within the body of the earth, within the astral plane, and within your very own physical temples, even within the motive of the heart. It takes an intense action of the violet light, or it takes a persistent year-by-year action of the violet light.

The question that arises, then, beloved ones, is: What of those souls who are of God and yet who respond to the discordant chords of rebellion within themselves?

Those who originate in God's light, who are the children of the light who respond to the seeds of Lucifer within themselves, need the miracle dissolving action of the violet flame. And yet by the very presence of those seeds of rebellion within them, they do not endure. They do not persist in the giving of the dynamic decrees that would ultimately cause the dissolution of those momentums within them.

And therefore many have left and gone their way because they were not content, having within them the sown seeds of discontent. They were not content to tarry with the LORD, to tarry with the Guru, to tarry with the Lord Christ, and to receive that miracle not by sudden transmutation but by a gradual transmutation.

It is to the children of the light that I direct your attention—counselors, teachers, representatives of truth, you who have a greater vision than they have because you have persisted, not necessarily forever and a day but for a number of years in this very process.

And when you have encountered the momentums of deception within yourself and you have seen those momentums of rebellion, you have hung on. You have known that the light of the ascended masters was greater than your own, and you were willing to trust. And therefore you became a focus of trust in the Guru-chela relationship. And when your power was not great enough to defeat the Adversary within you, you had the power of the Great White Brotherhood to suddenly infuse your temple with light. For this is the service of the Guru.

And though your own momentum of the violet flame was not enough for the transmutation of that energy, yet those forcefields within you were set aside by the intercession of angels and seraphim and cherubim, whose faces you did not see but who stood with you, guarding the temple of being *because you kept the faith!* And therefore without faith it is impossible to please God[11] and to return to the dimension of harmony and alignment with your Inner Self.

Let Your Love Increase as You Behold Those in Need of the Violet Flame

Therefore some children of the light could not tarry. They could not stand the uncomfortability of the Adversary within the midst of their very own chakras, their very own subconscious. It is to these that we direct our attention, and we say to the body of light upon earth:

You who have seen beyond the hour of intense temptation, you who have won your certain victory and you who are set on the Path, come what may, you are the ones who must apply yourselves to an acceleration of the violet flame so that when you go forth two by two across the face of the earth and you see the eyes of a child of God peering at you from behind all of the effluvia of the world, you will be able to deliver the goods, as they say. You will be able to deliver a momentum of violet flame that comes from the very heart of Saint Germain and the causal bodies of the ascended masters, as well as your own causal body of light.

And that sudden, intense transfer of light is the very meaning of the presence of the messenger in your midst, for this is often the only action of the Law that will be for the saving of a soul. Thus has God ordained his offices in hierarchy—his apostles and ministers and disciples and chelas, each one carrying that increment of light that is a sufficient grace unto their individual assignment in the order of hierarchy.

Now let your love increase as you behold those in need of

the great miracle of Saint Germain's violet flame. And let your love be a manifest action of giving those dynamic decrees as though you meant it and as though the world depended upon your giving of those decrees. [See inset "Decrees & the Science of the Spoken Word," pp. 110–15.]

Wake Up, O Children of God Who Have Gone Astray!

Wake up, I say! *Wake up,* O children of God who have gone astray! *Wake up* now and know that all of your criticism and condemnation and judgment and all of your gossip and all of your backsliding and all of your suspicions regarding the messenger or the chelas or the organization deprive you of communion with the great hierarchy that is just beyond the veil.

The veil is so thin, my beloved, that it is a wonder that you do not feel the great heat of the sacred fire literally lapping at your heart and at your chakras, ready to enter when you reenter into that blessed communion of the body and blood of God.

Accelerate the Light of the Seven Rays

My beloved, understand that the nine gifts of the Holy Spirit have to do with a similar acceleration of the light of the seven rays within you and ultimately of the action of Alpha and Omega in the white-fire core of being.

As you garner the momentum of the blue ray, so will you build a magnet in your aura that magnetizes the great light of your causal body. And the blue power of God that descends is for the exorcism of demons and discarnates by the authority of the Word, by the power of God. And that same sword of Kali,[12] that same blue energy, establishes God-government and realigns the nations of the earth under the flame of the government of Alpha and Omega.

And therefore you who have made your invocations to Mighty

Astrea[13] are building a great central sun magnet in your own heart flame of the white light of purity, of the blue ray. And thus the twofold action of Serapis and Morya comes more and more into your grasp, and now you must begin to exercise the authority commensurate with the light that you evoke from God.

The Children of God Must Be Healed of the Vibration of Rebellion

See, then, how the gift of healing, which is the counterpart of the gift of miracles, is also necessary so that there will be a healing of the consciousness of the children of God. The children of God must be *healed* of the vibration of rebellion! I say, *healed!* And I say, *you* must be the instruments of God's healing, for God is the only healer!

Pursue the gift of healing! Understand that it consists of truth—truth that is defended, that is spoken, a truth unto which you witness, truth as the purity of the All-Seeing Eye of God that casts out first your own self-deceptions, that casts out your inability to see life and to understand what is happening in the earth. Truth is a mighty flame. It becomes the servant of those who serve it, even as the fiery salamanders [of the elemental kingdom] are the servants of those who serve the sacred fire.

If you would have truth serve you, if you would earn the great gift of healing as a divine art, you must understand that there can be no compromise with truth. For the truth that makes you free is a science, and the science of God is heavy with the power of God.

The Casting of the Bread upon the Waters

Look at the science of energy as you survey the mountains— the fire in the heart of the mountains, the fire in the heart of the molecules of the sea and the air and the stars. Why, the universe is literally brimming with energy to which mankind have little or no access whatsoever because they have not passed the initiations of the great Tree of Life or of the Mystery School.

Our circle of fire *is* a circle of fire, and it remains a circle of fire! Our purpose is set! Our purpose is to publish the teachings, which can be partaken of morsel by morsel as crumbs from the masters' table by the children of God upon earth.

Each morsel that they eat as the published word—a book or a tape or a decree or a poem or a song—becomes the body and blood of Christ, which accelerates their own auric forcefield just a little bit more so that each time they partake of a morsel, they too can contain more light until they may make the decision to step once again into the circle of fire, where the great intensity of the LORD God is dispensed unto the chelas of this age.

Therefore the casting of the bread upon the waters is the casting of the bread of the Garden of Eden, the very initiations of Maitreya that go out upon the whole earth. And one book becomes a sword that divides the way of Light and Darkness and demands the choice. And with the choice is the judgment.

The book is the very person of myself. The tape is the person of the ascended master who is speaking. Wherever they fall as manna upon the children of Israel, so that manna becomes the catalyst of the leavening of the body of God, and so morsel by morsel they approach the living flame. Some may not arrive in this life, some may not see the Promised Land, and some may not regain entrance into the temples of Lemuria. But because you have kept the flame, they will be a little bit closer. They will have advanced on the spiral of life.

They will have advanced, and therefore in succeeding lifetimes they will come to the place where they *dare* to walk in the footsteps of the avatars who have gone before them. This is not the work of a day or a decade. It is the work of the millennia! Millennia are lost by the rebellion of the one and the few, and those millennia must be regained step-by-step and spiral by spiral. If it could be otherwise, I assure you that the Lord God would have provided the means. But he has not, because of the great energy that in its power is able to create, to preserve, or to destroy life.

Seek the Attainment of the Mighty Flow of God

Let God consciousness increase within you. Let the seriousness of the relationship to the ascended masters be upon you. Let your awareness of this reality make you willing to defend the honor—the honor that is even now Excalibur[14] held by El Morya within your midst, that mighty sword gainst which the sun of Helios and Vesta[15] reflects the blinding light.

The blinding light is the energy of your very own being. So that sword Excalibur represents honor—an honor that will not be silenced, that will not be put back or put down. And those who would carry the sword in El Morya's name must be willing to uphold the reality of the Guru-chela relationship in an hour when it is threatened by the very ones whom I, Maitreya, cast out of the Garden of Eden.

Thousands upon thousands were cast out of the early Mystery School. Even as God cast them out of heaven, so the rebellious ones were cast out of Lemuria until their rebellion was so great that God withdrew the entire platform itself and allowed the Mystery School to ascend into the etheric plane, where only the elect might enter.

Those very ones cast out of that relationship of love are the ones who persecute the lightbearers today. I say: *They* shall not pass! *They* shall not cross the circle of fire! *They* shall not put down the great light of the teaching as long as there is one chela upon earth who is Father, Son, and Holy Ghost incarnate.

How many of you can claim that attainment at this moment? If you cannot, then it is a goal that you can achieve, not because of yourself but because God has ordained it and because you attain it by the grace of the eternal Guru who lives in you, your own beloved Christ Self.

Seek, then, the attainment of the mighty flow of God and hear as I speak that message that even Kuthumi desires to deliver to you, and even Djwal Kul and even El Morya as they continue to unveil the most profound and scientific studies of the human aura become the divine aura.[16]

Hear, then, the great mystery of the cyclings of the rings of your causal body. How many figure-eight flows are contained within you? Do you know, O chela, how many cyclings of that great mystical figure-eight sign are passing through you in this hour?

You visualize one, and within one are a million times one, as each and every unique frequency of your own causal body passes over another pattern, another design of the figure eight. Oh, the science of God, the immensity of that science!

The Fallen Ones' Vengeance against God

Yet—*yet* those fallen ones who went out from the very throne of Alpha and Omega in defiance came to the earth. They gave to the children of men the secrets of God whereby the children of men began to practice their manipulations and their sorceries on elemental life and their imprisonment of elemental life and their creations—horrendous creations that were desecrations of God.

You see, the fallen ones, in their vengeance against God, said, "We will whisper the mysteries into the ears of mortals, and the mortals will then abuse the mysteries. They will sin against God and then they will bear the karma of that sin"—always calculating to have another one bear the burden of their own disobedience.

And so the children of men gathered in their covens, in their rituals, in imitation of the great solar rings and of the great rituals of the mighty seraphim.

And therefore God withdrew from the earth and I withdrew from Eden and from the giving of the mysteries, lest they should be passed on to those who had not the commitment of the inner flame. But the pulsation and the transfer of the mind of God have never been withdrawn from the son and daughter of God. It has been spoken in a whisper in the secret chamber of the heart, and only the souls who have entered that secret chamber in meditation have received the holy oil of initiation and of the inner teaching.

The fallen ones sought to subvert the very mystery of creation itself by their insubordination, but God knew from the beginning that he had not entrusted his ultimate secrets unto those who might yet turn against the light. And thus you come to understand why the mysteries we deliver are kernels of light that must be warmed by an accelerated devotion to the threefold flame so that the shell of the kernel might be broken and the soul eat of the meat of the Word contained within.

We Are Bringing You to the Communion of Your Own Heart

Our emphasis upon devotion, upon the dynamic decrees, and upon the simple truths is our understanding whereby we are bringing you to the communion of your own heart, where the mysteries revealed remain sealed within your soul, sometimes even sealed from your outer mind. Even while your inner soul is evolving and transcending and attaining heights of cosmic consciousness, the outer mind remains seemingly simple, perhaps rough-hewn and uneducated, as were the great fishermen and the others whom Christ called to be his disciples.

So then, God protects the mystery of the Holy Grail. Even as his face was veiled in the Holy of Holies, so the veiling of the mysteries is a protection unto all life, the life that is God.

Many of you contain inner mysteries, which in their outworkings in your life produce a magnificence of service. Understand that God holds each chela in the hollow of his hand. And by your faithfulness your attainment is won in an inner sense, even while you sometimes wonder about the outwardness of your appearance and your seeming lack of outer knowledge.

God has sealed you in a mystery, and the Great White Brotherhood tenderly cares for the sheep of the Great Shepherd. That you might pass through the door of the ascension and open that door wider for the evolutions of light is our prayer.

I Call the Faithful to Be Initiated

I, Maitreya, come. And the cornucopia that God has given to me is so full of the fruits of the Spirit, which I desire to deliver to you, that I would tarry with you the afternoon, if it were possible for you to endure so much light. But because the Great Law will not allow it, I therefore come to the seminar and deliver to you for a weekend the musings of my heart.[17]

I call the faithful to be initiated, to come to Camelot, to come to the Mystery School of Eden, and then to unite in the one mighty flame of the Cosmic Christ the acceleration of that wisdom of the mind of God, to unite in the great energy of the second ray of wisdom and to feel that ray of light in all of its transforming, radiating spirals of light.

I come to prepare your temples for the greater light of the resurrection of your memory of God. I come, then, to anoint you. And I come this day to Summit University to also announce the implementation of your greater integration—Spirit and Matter,

Alpha and Omega—which can only be accomplished by your entering into a sacred labor through the Holy Ghost.

You have heard the law of the Father and the wisdom of the Son. I call you then to an active interpenetration with the Holy Ghost. I call you to a service within our community of the Holy Spirit. This week, then, we shall implement that plan, that divine plan of God whereby you will take your place side by side with chelas who are chelas because they are God in action, because they are implementing the Word in a service that instantaneously blesses every part of life.

The very service of this community to the body of God upon earth is a miracle in itself. And when you think even of the delivery of the weekly *Pearls of Wisdom,*[18] you also see the instantaneous transmutation by the gift of miracles, which occurs as a sphere of light is deposited in the heart of all who read those *Pearls.* In some, it is the judgment of impure motive. In others it is the judgment of purity of heart and a resurrection unto eternal life.

I stand in the nation America. And Enoch walks to expose the true and the false teachers and to restore this nation to sanity, to health, cell by cell. Let our chelas continue to be an infusion, a veritable transfusion of the blood and the body of the Lord Christ for the holding of the balance in an hour of transition.

I AM Maitreya. *They shall not pass!*

February 4, 1979
Camelot
Los Angeles County, California

THE CHART OF YOUR DIVINE SELF

The Chart of Your Divine Self

Is God really so far from us, as many people have come to believe?

In eternity and in the one flame of life, there is only one God. As we inhabit the dimensions of time and space, we can conceive of this God as very personal, very intimate, very close to us. The God to whom we speak, who answers our prayers, who speaks back to us, who comforts us in our aloneness—this is the individualization of God. That same one God can be speaking simultaneously to billions of lifewaves, but for the purpose of the organization of the energies of cosmos, that sphere, that identity of God, is individualized and focalized where we are.

If you take a drop of water from the ocean and put it in on your finger, you will see that the drop is quite small. But all of the elements that make up the ocean can be found in that single drop of water. Your soul is a drop in the vast ocean of Being, a cell in the body of God. The profound truth is that out of his great love for us, God has placed his very essence within each one. This reality is demonstrated in the Chart of Your Divine Self.

This Chart is the unique outline of your inner identity, showing three levels of being, from the human to the divine. It explains how Spirit becomes Matter within you, how you can move from the midst of your everyday life to the heights of union with God. Many of the cosmic truths discovered by the great mystics and teachers of East and West throughout history are depicted in this Chart.

The Upper Figure

The upper figure in the Chart is the individualization of God's presence for every son and daughter of his heart, which we call your mighty I AM God Presence, or I AM Presence. It is your *personalized* I AM THAT I AM, the name that God revealed to Moses at Mount Sinai when God said, "This is my name forever and this is my memorial unto all generations."* To Hindus it is Brahma,

---
*Exod. 3:14, 15

Buddhists call it the Dharmakaya, while Christians think of it as God the Father. Whenever we say the words, "I AM," we are really saying "God in me is."

The I AM THAT I AM is the one God, and yet it is individualized for each of us. It is the drop in the ocean. It is really not separate, and yet it is separate. It is apart from God, and yet never apart from God. For the purposes of relating time and space to infinity, we talk about the I AM Presence. Yet it is not a symbol. It is a reality. It is more real than anything we have ever experienced. It is our true, Divine Selfhood.

The I AM Presence is surrounded by colored spheres of light that comprise the causal body, depicted in the Chart as colored rings. This is the body of First Cause, which contains within it man's "treasures laid up in heaven"*—words and works, thoughts and feelings of virtue, attainment, and light—pure energies that you have expressed in this and past lifetimes as the result of the judicious exercise of free will. It is like your cosmic bank account.

We might think that when we pass from this lifetime we lose all of the talents and qualities that we have gained, but this is not so. All of the good karma we have made since our soul's descent into Matter also rises to this body and multiplies our inherent talents, strengths, and gifts. When we tap into the energy in our causal body, it is released to us as blessing, bounty, wisdom, light, love, and direction.

The Middle Figure

The great avatars of all ages who have come to liberate us have been the full embodiment of the middle figure, and they have been greatly overshadowed by, and many times been bonded to, the upper figure in the Chart. Therefore they have walked the earth with the shining halo of their own causal body, such as the Buddhas who embody the Dharmakaya, the I AM Presence.

This middle figure in the Chart is the figure of the Inner Christ or the Inner Buddha. It is the body of your higher consciousness,

---

*Matt. 6:19–21

your higher mind, your higher knowing, your higher intuition, your inner teacher. This teacher is called your Holy Christ Self or your Holy Buddha Self. Some Christian mystics have referred to it as the inner man of the heart. It is referred to here as the Christ Self, the inner Christ within our heart. We also refer to it as the Higher Self. Buddhists call this the Sambhogakaya.

The word *Christ* comes from the Greek word *Christos,* which means "anointed." This middle figure represents the office of the Christ, a certain level of God consciousness to which we can all attain. The Chart of Your Divine Self shows a picture of Jesus as an example of one who has attained this level of Christhood. At a spiritual level, the Christian concept of accepting Christ as one's Saviour or into one's life or heart is actually the accepting of this middle figure.

The Christ Self is sometimes called the Mediator because it is the go-between—the one mediating between your evolving soul consciousness (the lower figure in the Chart) and the God consciousness of the I AM THAT I AM. By following the path of initiation, you can gradually become one with that teacher and walk the earth in that level of consciousness, anointed with the light of your I AM Presence.

The Lower Figure

The lower figure in the Chart represents your soul clothed in a physical body as it evolves in time and space and learns the lessons of love and mastery. Buddhists call this the Nirmanakaya, the place where transformation and change take place.

The light of God descends from your I AM Presence to your Christ Self and then to your soul over what is called the crystal cord, or silver cord. This light of God, this spark of divinity, is anchored within the secret chamber of the heart, which is called the *Ananda-Kanda* in Sanskrit, "the root of joy."

This spark of divinity within you is called the threefold flame because it has three "plumes" that embody the three primary attributes of the love, wisdom, and power of God. It is the very point where God's energy in Spirit becomes God's energy in

Matter within you. As the light of God descends according to your soul's desire, there is an increase in your holy love, wisdom, and power, or strength, to help you navigate through the entanglements of karmic existence and to rise to higher levels of awareness of the Christ within.

Therefore, right within your heart there is a point of contact with the Divine, a flame from God's own heart given to his sons and daughters of light! It is your soul's point of contact with the Supreme Source of all life! This is great news!

The Tube of Light

In this lower figure in the Chart, the soul is standing in a pillar of light called the tube of light. The tube of light is an electronic forcefield that descends from the heart of your I AM Presence and surrounds your Christ Self and your soul, and it seals and protects you from all that is less than the Christ consciousness. This tube of light will be sustained for twenty-four hours as long as you guard it with harmony in your thoughts, feelings, words, and deeds.

You can visualize this tube of light as the dazzling white light of your I AM Presence, brighter than the sun shining on new-fallen snow, coalescing as a cylinder of light around you. You can visualize it as being about nine feet in diameter, extending from approximately nine feet above you to about three feet beneath your feet.

You can also visualize the violet flame surrounding you within the tube of light. [See inset "The Sacred Gift of the Violet Flame" on pp. 117–21.] As long as our soul has karma and is still working toward union with our Christ Self and I AM Presence, we have impurities and imperfections. So we need the violet flame within the tube of light to carry on the continuous process of transmutation.

You will see that just above the head of the Christ Self is the dove of the Holy Spirit descending from God. This signifies that the divine Comforter tends to each of us as we face the spiritual tests and trials that come our way. As the Holy Spirit comes into our life, there comes to us a great feeling of oneness with all life, of being at home in the universe. It is the energy of the currents of life, of the essence of God himself made personal for each of us.

The following is a prayer that you can give daily to anchor the light of your I AM Presence, your Holy Christ Self, the violet flame, and the tube of light into your world, right where you are!

VIOLET FIRE AND TUBE OF LIGHT DECREE
by the Ascended Master Saint Germain

O my constant, loving I AM Presence, thou Light of God above me whose radiance forms a circle of fire before me to light my way:

I AM faithfully calling to thee to place a great pillar of Light from my own mighty I AM God Presence all around me right now today! Keep it intact through every passing moment, manifesting as a shimmering shower of God's beautiful Light through which nothing human can ever pass. Into this beautiful electric circle of divinely charged energy direct a swift upsurge of the violet fire of Freedom's forgiving, transmuting flame!

Cause the ever expanding energy of this flame projected downward into the forcefield of my human energies to completely change every negative condition into the positive polarity of my own Great God Self! Let the magic of its mercy so purify my world with Light that all whom I contact shall always be blessed with the fragrance of violets from God's own heart in memory of the blessed dawning day when all discord—cause, effect, record, and memory—is forever changed into the Victory of Light and the peace of the ascended Jesus Christ.

I AM now constantly accepting the full power and manifestation of this fiat of Light and calling it into instantaneous action by my own God-given free will and the power to accelerate without limit this sacred release of assistance from God's own heart until all men are ascended and God-free in the Light that never, never, never fails!

Decrees & the Science of the Spoken Word

Spoken prayer is at the heart of the world's religions East and West, whether it is the Jewish Shema and Amidah, the Christian Lord's Prayer, or the Buddhist Om Mani Padme Hum.

These traditional prayers rely on principles used in ancient civilizations that have been passed down through the ages. The ascended masters have since expounded on these principles so that we can use them more effectively for personal and world change in what is known as the science of the spoken Word.

The science of the spoken Word can be considered a step-up of all prayer forms of East and West. It includes prayers, fiats, mantras, affirmations, and decrees.

THE THROAT CHAKRA

A decree is more than a request. It is a command, which can be short or long. It is a carefully worded spiritual formula whereby the consciousness of God enters into our world. In fact, unlocking the energies of your Higher Self is the goal of the effective use of the spoken Word. And you will never know just how much light you can actually draw down until you try.*

The Call Compels the Answer

There is a cosmic law that states, "The call compels the answer." So when you give a decree, energy *must* respond and the universe *must* answer your call according to God's will.

When we decree, we are directing light into our world. We are commanding the flow of energy from Spirit to Matter. This is what God asked us to do when he said through the prophet Isaiah, "Ask me of things to come concerning my sons, and concerning the work of my hands, command ye me."† It has also been said, "Thou shalt make the prayer unto him, and he shall hear thee. . . . Thou shalt also decree a thing, and it shall be established unto thee."‡

It takes this understanding to use the science of the spoken Word effectively. This is a sacred science whereby we voluntarily enter into a partnership and become co-creators with God, and the mediator of this co-creation is always our Higher Self.

The power of our request for any change lies in how we ask and the words we speak. When we say the name of God I AM THAT I AM, which was given to Moses, we are declaring, "God in me is." The "I" who is speaking is not the lesser self but the Greater Self. God within is saying, "I AM THAT I AM." For who but God within has the authority to declare being, consciousness, Self-awareness? It is an affirmation of our true spiritual being. It releases the fire of our heart to fulfill the purpose to which we send it forth. When we say the name of God I AM THAT I AM, we are affirming our inner reality.

---

*Also see teachings on decrees to the violet flame in the inset, "The Sacred Gift of the Violet Flame," pp. 117–21.
†Isa. 45:11
‡Job 22:27, 28

Let There Be Light!

The first decree ever recorded was spoken by God: "Let there be light!"* and instantaneously there *was* light. The response to the decree of the Word sent forth by God was Creation itself!

The gift of speech is the empowerment to create and to bless all life by the masterful use of the Word. Without it, we would be powerless to invoke light and divine assistance. When Jesus raised Lazarus from the dead, he employed this power to release energy from the plane of Spirit to the plane of Matter in order to restore the life of Lazarus. It is recorded that "he cried with a loud voice" when he gave the command, "Lazarus, come forth!"†

Decrees are spoken because it is the power of the Word that is able to create, to preserve, to uncreate, and to perfect the divine image within us. Therefore, decrees should always be given aloud if possible.

The following is an example of a simple decree that affirms the light within:

Light, set me free! Light, set me free! Light, set me free!
Light command, Light command,
   Light command, command, command!
Light demand, Light demand, Light demand, demand, demand!
Light expand, Light expand, Light expand, expand, expand!
Light I AM, Light I AM, Light I AM, I AM, I AM!
I AM a being of Violet Fire,
I AM the Purity God desires.

Whenever you give a decree, the light that is flowing through you is stamped with the divine pattern of that decree. Repeating decrees is a ritual that stamps more of your energy with that same divine pattern.

Repeating decrees is not "vain repetition" but scientific repetition, because we know exactly what we are doing. We are consciously commanding that energy to flow.

---
*Gen. 1:3
†John 11:43

Decree Every Day

It is beneficial to decree every day because the spiritual light you invoke naturally seeks its own level. So in each twenty-four hours, we pray and decree again to draw the light down into our world in order to assist with our life and to balance the day's karma.

The best time to do this is early in the morning when things are peaceful, because at the hour of dawn your karma for that day, good or bad, is delivered to you. Doing your decrees early can also help transform what could have been a chaotic day, when everything is coming at you, into a day when things are flowing smoothly. Starting your day with decrees can help you rise above inevitable challenges as well as the traps of negative karma.

Start with Spiritual Protection

When you begin your decree session, it is important to start with the light of spiritual protection. In our everyday lives we recognize that we need protection for ourselves, our loved ones, our community, and our world. We also need protection from negative energies that can affect our moods, health, and overall well-being.

Archangel Michael is the angel of protection. He is the greatest and most revered angel in Jewish, Christian, and Islamic traditions and is called by many different names. Michael is the archangel of the blue ray of protection, faith, and God's will. Along with the legions of angels under his command, he protects us from physical and spiritual dangers.

When you need protection right away, you can just make a fervent call, "Archangel Michael, help me, help me, help me!" You can also ask him to protect your loved ones and others, including all souls on earth.

We often begin a decree by saying, "In the name of my beloved I AM Presence and Holy Christ Self," as in the short "Traveling Protection" decree below. When we say this, we are decreeing by the authority of God within us.

This authority comes from the light of God within us, which is the spark of life called the threefold flame anchored in the secret chamber of the heart of the souls of light. This "divine spark" is your soul's point of contact with the Supreme Source of all life, as seen in the lower figure in the Chart of Your Divine Self.

You can give the following decree every morning to protect you throughout the day, wherever you go. It is a good decree to give when driving or traveling. You can repeat verses as many times as you like, remembering that the more times you say them, the more light you draw down.

After you've finished the decree, you can accept what you've called for by sealing it with a short call of acceptance like the one below. You may also use this closing at the end of any decree to anchor the light you have invoked into this physical world. We always add "according to the will of God" so that we don't inadvertently request something that may be our desire but isn't God's desire.

TRAVELING PROTECTION

In the name of my beloved I AM Presence and Holy Christ Self, I decree:

Lord Michael before, Lord Michael behind,
Lord Michael to the right, Lord Michael to the left,
Lord Michael above, Lord Michael below,
Lord Michael, Lord Michael wherever I go!

I AM his Love protecting here!
I AM his Love protecting here!
I AM his Love protecting here! (3x)

And in full faith I consciously accept this manifest in full power according to God's will.

Affirm the Light of God within You

The following is a beautiful decree for anchoring the light of God right where you are:

I AM LIGHT
by Kuthumi

I AM Light, glowing Light,
Radiating Light, intensified Light.
God consumes my darkness,
Transmuting it into Light.

This day I AM a focus of the Central Sun.
Flowing through me is a crystal river,
A living fountain of Light
That can never be qualified
By human thought and feeling.
I AM an outpost of the Divine.
Such darkness as has used me is swallowed up
By the mighty river of Light which I AM.

I AM, I AM, I AM Light;
I live, I live, I live in Light.
I AM Light's fullest dimension;
I AM Light's purest intention.
I AM Light, Light, Light
Flooding the world everywhere I move,
Blessing, strengthening, and conveying
The purpose of the kingdom of heaven.

The Sacred Gift of the Violet Flame

If we ask ourselves what the biggest impediment is to our entering into the path of initiation with Lord Maitreya, the answer will likely be the need to forgive ourselves for some past misdeed or to forgive another person for wrongs they have done to us.

We have had many lifetimes and have been in many situations that have caused us great pain, regret, and nonresolution—whether our fault or another's—and this is a weight upon our soul that needs to be cleared in order for us to be free.

The question we might then ask is: How can we clear up these karmic burdens and achieve our soul's victory, while also not adding more karma from one embodiment to the next?

Saint Germain has given us the answer to this question, which is that we can clear our past karma through the use of the violet flame—by invoking the light of love, forgiveness, mercy, transmutation, and alchemy, which brings our soul into alignment with God's desire and plan for us. These are the gifts of the violet flame.

The Violet Flame Can Clear Past-Life Records

We know that we can pray for the healing of an ailment, for the protection from harm, for wisdom in solving a difficult problem, all of which are answered through the love of God according to his will.

But have we known that there is a powerful light we can invoke in order to specifically clear ourselves from past-life records, hurt, or hardness of heart? We might think of these negative energies as a molasses that "gum up" our physical, emotional, mental, and spiritual bodies, which can affect our health and spiritual well-being. The violet flame dissolves these energies and gives us a positive spin.

The violet flame has tremendous power to improve our lives because it is a high-frequency light that spans physical and spiritual realms. It is a vibrant spiritual light that transmutes energy from its current state into a higher one. It is the spiritual light of alchemy that produces positive change.

If you've ever studied the beautiful rainbows that sometimes appear right after it rains, you may have noticed that the violet seems to trail off into infinity, as though there were more to the rainbow than the physical eye can see. The color violet disappears into a higher frequency violet ray, forming a bridge between the physical world and the spiritual world.

The violet light has the shortest wavelength and the highest frequency of visible light. Just like the violet color in nature's rainbow, this high-frequency violet light can be understood as a point of transition from the visible to the invisible, from the physical plane to the spiritual plane. To the ancient mystics and alchemists, this transitional color was a spiritual rather than a physical phenomenon.

The Violet Flame Allows Us to Transcend Ourselves

The violet flame is the alchemical action of transmutation that allows us to transcend ourselves. The Word *transmutation* means changing something into a higher form and was used by alchemists who attempted to "transmute" base metals into gold, separating the "subtle" from the "gross" by means of heat. For ancient and medieval alchemists, the real purpose of alchemical transmutation was spiritual transformation.

The violet flame works at spiritual levels, permeating every cell and atom of our body, mind, emotions, and memories. When the violet flame comes into our world, it begins at the surface and then goes deeper and deeper. It can penetrate the most secret places of the mind and memory, even at subconscious and unconscious levels. It goes in, sweeps through, and cleans out the "dust" of centuries, restoring the natural flow of light within you.

From a spiritual perspective, when the atoms of our consciousness become clogged by the negative karma that's like dust under the bed, it slows down the vibration of the electrons. As the electrons slow down, our rate of vibration lowers. We become more burdened, and we begin to resonate more with negativity and less with pure, positive energy.

When the violet flame is invoked, it can literally consume the debris around our chakras. Using the violet flame is like soaking our chakras in a chemical solution that dissolves, layer by layer, the negative karmic substance that has been trapped there for perhaps thousands of years.

The violet flame is the memory of the perfection of what should be—in everyone, everything, every place, and every circumstance. When we ask for this violet fire to move into action, it raises the vibrations of all it contacts until divine order is brought into manifestation through its merciful, forgiving, and transforming power of divine love. Thus, the alchemical transformation brought by the violet flame will move you and all life ever toward perfection.

Saint Germain Revealed the Knowledge of the Violet Flame

The violet flame is not something new. It is the light of the Holy Spirit. Some saints and mystics have noted in their biographies that when they reached a certain point in their inner communion, they began to see a violet light and to experience the infilling of their being with the Spirit during prayer and meditation. In previous centuries, knowledge of the violet flame was taught only to a chosen few who had proven themselves worthy.

The violet flame was not revealed to the masses until the 1930s, when Saint Germain released this knowledge to the world through the I AM Activity. Mark L. Prophet and Elizabeth Clare Prophet received further revelations on the violet flame since the founding of The Summit Lighthouse in 1958, and they have spread the understanding of its use to many people of light worldwide.

Many who use the violet flame are students on various spiritual paths East and West. Using the violet flame helps you to be a better seeker of truth, a better Christian, a better Jew, a better Buddhist, a better Hindu, a better Muslim. Why? Because no matter what your beliefs, the violet flame universally helps clear the way for you to follow your chosen path more effectively.

You Can Access the Violet Flame Anytime and Anywhere

We've all had times when we have sought help from a Higher Source, whether we call that Source God, Jesus, Buddha, the Great Spirit, Allah, or the universe. Our request might be as simple as "O God, help me!" So when you need the violet flame, you might say a quick call, like "O God, please send violet flame into this situation now!"

You can access the violet flame anytime and anywhere through prayers, mantras, and visualizations. A sincere call or prayer made with a loving heart always works. When you want the action of the violet flame in your life, you can simply ask for it, say a prayer for it, recite a mantra, or give a quick and clear request for what you need.

Here is a violet-flame mantra to help get you started. You can use it every time you have a spare minute, repeating it as many times as you would like.

As you say this mantra, visualize the violet flame bathing and cleansing your aura. See the flames dissolve the debris in and around it. You are saying, "I AM the purity God desires!" because you want to purify your aura of everything that is not of God. You can visualize any negative energy that contacts these flames being instantaneously transmuted into the light of God. The daily use of the power of the spoken Word combined with visualization is an unbeatable formula!

> I AM a being of violet fire!
> I AM the purity God desires!

When you give this mantra, you are using the name of God I AM THAT I AM, which was given to Moses. Every time you say, "I AM" you are declaring, "God in me is." "God in me is a being of violet fire! God in me is the purity God desires!" It is an affirmation of your true spiritual being. It releases the fire of your heart to fulfill the purpose to which we send it forth. This is more than the power of positive thinking. It is the alchemy of the sacred fire. When we take the name of God I AM THAT I AM, we are affirming our inner reality.

Here is one more mantra, also called a decree, to help get you started.

> Violet fire, thou love divine,
> Blaze within this heart of mine!
> Thou art mercy forever true,
> Keep me always in tune with you.

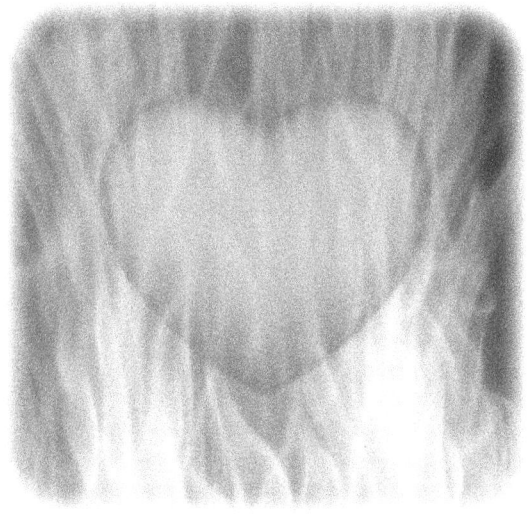

*I place myself at the goal of your life.
I AM Maitreya, the goalpost.
I AM Maitreya,
the beginning of the Word,
the ending of the Word.
If you think you are caught in the middle,
you are.*

CHAPTER 8

The Oscillation of Light for the Alignment of Your Soul

L ight out of the infinite sphere is the descent of Allness. But how can the smallness of the lesser self appropriate the light when it cannot equate itself with the All?

The lesser mind conceives itself to be in a level of attainment that it has in no wise gained, for the lesser self is incapable of that attainment. But the soul—the soul rising in the spirals of the resurrection current—is able to be God in proportion to its ability to assimilate God.

Now, some have concluded that they have concluded a course of study with Maitreya.[1] But I say, you have scarcely crossed the threshold of the ascended masters' university. I come, then, to impart reality, not alone to you but to our chelas positioned here and there in the circles of the earth.

I AM the Buddha in the midst of the fiery core of the lotus. I step down the great spheres of Gautama. I translate his peace into levels of initiation.

I AM the transcendent one. Therefore, see translucent spheres of consciousness where I would bid you enter. But first I must know that you are divested of the momentums of Western civilization whereby all achievement is measured by outer conditions, outer manifestations, where those who have worked a certain spiral then consider that they have somehow earned a gift or earned a status in their community or their social level. Putting in time or putting in space, however, sometimes results in a minus-zero achievement as more is lost than is gained.

The Vulnerability of the Soul

I would not have you ignorant of your own personal need to pursue the Path with a diligence that you have not yet known or comprehended, and with a seriousness that can enter into the joy of the Lord and yet is never caught off guard.

Unbeknownst to you, as you have entered a path of independence you have entered a corresponding spiral of dependence. Now that you have had stripped from you the props of worldly manifestations, concealments, crutches you have borne, you are therefore more helpless in that world and therefore more dependent upon the reality of God than ever before since you were born. For you see, the lesser self has learned to protect itself by ways unlawful. When these dissolve, the corresponding shafts of light must be as tempered steel.

Why do you think so many are lost who enter the Path? It is because they have not understood co-measurement. They have not understood the vulnerability of the soul, now without the reinforcements of the human consciousness, the human defenses. I would not have you, then, as defenseless babes, but I would increase your dependence upon the God flame that I AM.

Wherefore has the Lord God appointed me initiator of your soul? It is because it is essential that I am with you alway,[2] even unto the end of the cycles of your human consciousness, which even now obliterates and confuses your own understanding of yourself.

You, then, have scarcely begun to understand the kindergarten of the Path under the Guru Maitreya. This is well worthy of praise, worthy of the acclamation of angels, but unworthy of a false self-esteem. Compared to the masses of the earth, you are in other realms apart. But looking upon the ladder of the ascension, you are as little children, scarcely able to place a foot upon the first rung of the ladder and hold it there without our strong arm and support.

Let chelas, then, not be emboldened by the comparison of the self to others upon earth or to other chelas of other schools. This is a most dangerous state of mind whereby you become overconfident because you have heard the Word without realizing that the hearing of the Word is not the translation of the soul until you experience and become the Word.

Be attentive, then, and think not that because you have advanced beyond your fellows you can now at will invoke the violet flame and your burdens and cares will pass away, that you can now scamper off to other areas and feel that because you have walked these halls you are somehow magically protected or magically sustained.

The Correct Assessment of Self

Beloved ones, the rigors of the Path are not made known but rather are concealed by the very temper and mood of Western civilization. You know not bodily hardships. You know not want. Scarcely are the sinews of the mind exercised, for all comes with the ease of a life pattern, which if it were the mastery of the abundant life it would be realistic, inasmuch as it is the building of a materialistic empire by souls of light. But ah, yes, [it is also built] by souls of darkness, who have known that to build such an empire is to leave souls off guard who can scarcely understand that they themselves are yet helpless before the elements of nature, helpless before the great oncoming law of karma.

I come, then, to pull you into alignment by a sudden and severe awareness of your own impoverished consciousness and the disciplines that I expect you shall engage in, body and soul and mind.

Mighty Victory[3] has surveyed the lightbearers of this first class of initiation at Summit University[4] and he has said to me, "O Maitreya, most holy one, souls of light are as babes dancing in the sparkling waters. They have not measured—no, they have not measured the battle and they are not ready to move with our legions. Therefore, let them not be disillusioned but let them be illumined to the necessities of a continuing pursuit of the light, no matter how painful, no matter how real."

Reality is a blazing sun from which you shield your eyes, yet one day you must face that sun. Therefore I come, O my beloved, to admonish you in the continuing of the law of love unto yourself, unto all around you.

I come not to crown you but to prepare you for the crown. I come, then, not to seal you but to unseal you. Therefore, let the substances of the chakras go into the flame. Let them be opened, and let light course through your veins.

You have only one body of peers. They are chelas on the path of Maitreya Buddha. They are in an etheric retreat, and there they receive the disciplines of the Law even as you are discovering those disciplines in the very life process of earth. For a comparison, then, of your progress, you may only be compared to those of equal karma, equal opportunity.

And therefore I say, it is necessary that you accelerate in order to be the counterpart of these chelas, who at inner levels hold a chalice of the wine of the Spirit that they would pour into your chalice. Co-measurement, balance, Alpha-Omega, let the inner and the outer chelas be one. Let their God flames commemorate their twin flames, and let earth be the biding place of heaven through your soul.

Watch and be vigilant, my beloved. Take the word of wisdom given to you, for we would call you the wise. To call you "the wise" is to bestow upon you the title of "sage." A sage is one who has the profound awareness of the path of chelaship. The sage is not the guru, but the sage has become a teacher of the teachings of the guru. The sage is one who is wise by co-measurement, by a correct assessment of the self.

I bid you to that inner discipline. I bid you to the calling. For the children of China are yearning for their sages to return, the children of India yearn for the Holy Mother, and the children of America await the sane word of the practical life of honor and love.

Trust Your Own Thread of Contact

I have positioned myself here at Camelot, and I sometimes sit as a peasant in the Mediterranean sun with my sombrero and my guitar. I pluck notes of ancient sounds, penetrating the depths of the subconscious.

I am here, and I extend my Electronic Presence to you. I challenge those areas that you would have challenged within your being—the hard-core awareness of self that is independent of God, a self-awareness of which you have scarcely an awareness at all.

Trust, then. O trust! Trust the dedication of the messenger and the Mystery School and your own garment, your own thread of contact. I place myself at the goal of your life. I AM Maitreya, the goalpost. I AM Maitreya, the beginning of the Word, the ending of the Word. If you think you are caught in the middle, you are.

And if sometimes you know not the way to turn or you are dizzy as though you had emerged from a merry-go-round and you think you are going to the goal when you are going to the source from whence you came, know, then, that from Alpha to Omega there is an arc of energy. You must become that arc. You must become that light.

> *O light! O light!*
> *O light invincible!*
> *O light within the heart!*
> *I AM the golden light of the arc.*
> *I AM Father and Mother.*
> *I AM the golden arc.*
> *I draw it through the heart.*

Now then, you, chela, move upon that thread from Father to Mother. And sometimes, as a little child pleads his case before Father and receives from Father the definite no, you then move along the arc of the thread to Mother and plead your case once more, hoping, hoping then to hear the definite yes.

Why, then, do the deliberations of Father and Mother sometimes differ? It is not our vacillation. It is because sometimes your energies are unacceptable to the plus polarity of being and therefore you cannot approach the energy of Father, and Father may not sponsor you in your endeavor. But out of your alignment with the Mother you then enter her heart and receive her sponsorship as intermediary of the throne of grace.

Now understand that your movement from the beginning to the ending and the ending to the beginning is the oscillation of light for the alignment of your soul in the Alpha and the Omega. And therefore your four lower bodies must be created and re-created, born and reborn, formed, unformed, and reformed, so that the spherical union may appear.

When you have penetrated all of Father that you can contain, then it is time for the balancing of polarity in Mother. These initiations come under the twelve hierarchies of the sun,[5] whom I represent to you. For, behold, I stand at the twelve gates of the New Jerusalem.[6] I stand at the portal of the cycle of your year of victory.

> *Alpha and Omega, for the alignment of the soul in the
>   initiations of the twelve hierarchies of the sun,
> I AM come to the altar of the Holy Grail.[7]
> I AM come for the raising up of Alpha and Omega within
>   these souls.
> I AM come, then, to initiate the cycle of Capricorn,
>   of the Great Divine Director,
>   of the light of Alpha and Omega within that open door
>   of Being.
> I AM that light of Being.
> I AM that light of Being.
> I AM that light of Being.
> I AM the open door of light.
> Therefore, let the soul pursue the essence of the Father-Mother God.
> Let that which has become the hard-core rebellion against that
>   light now face the eternal Sun.
> And let the soul in all courage be willing now to place that
>   substance into the flame, to become a spherical reality of
>   Being, a white sphere of light that is the golden sun held in
>   the hands of Maitreya.
> I AM Maitreya.
> I AM the Law of the One.
> I AM the Law of the One.
> I AM the Law of the One.
> I AM that flaming Presence of Being.*

Light out of the Great Central Sun,
Light out of the Great Central Sun, I release thy flame.
Light out of the Great Pyramid, I release thy flame.
Light out of the great sphere, I release thy flame.
Light out of the cosmic ovoid, the Cosmic Egg, I release thy flame.
Aim Aim Aim[8] [10-second pause]

Understand the Malintent of the Evil One

My beloved, your hearts have prepared for a greater light than you have ever known. Understand that a single raindrop contains within itself more energy than you have ever known. And therefore do not compliment yourself upon the receipt of the raindrop, but understand that you must summon a cosmos of God-control to be able to contain the energy locked within the raindrop of my soul.

Therefore, simply because you receive a greater light, do not rest content. For there are hordes of darkness waiting at the gate who have misqualified that quantity of light over a million years of duration of their vanity. They understand a co-measurement that you do not. Thus their leader entrapped the Goddess of Light in an hour of greater attainment than you now know.[9]

O beloved ones, remember, then, the story that is a history of those fallen ones imprisoning that one who had already sustained life in the physical temple for hundreds of years. And yet in a moment of indiscretion she was imprisoned in the body of a fish, in the lower half of that body, for that fish body could not go past the heart chakra.

Therefore, the requirement was to sustain life in that form for over eight hundred years before the ascension was given, because the light of that body had been raised to such a degree that the ascension was required from that point, even though the curse of the black magician had fallen upon it.

Understand these disciplines. Understand the malintent of the Evil One,[10] and understand that the single drop of light that I have invoked is great enough for the quaking of worlds. The fallen ones would take that light, and some among you know not the beginning of wisdom.[11]

Let it be, then, the constant prayer, the vigil of constancy, and the awareness that a planet is being infused with light and that many are they whose hatred of your light is unto the death.

Our joy is in the final victory. Our rejoicing on the way is the hallelujah of the risen Christ.

Let us be up and doing. Let us be in action. Let us see the hour of need. Let us fill that need.

The Hour Is Come for the Judgment

O Helios and Vesta, O Helios and Vesta, thy light is a brilliant star! We now face the karma of those who have lightly taken our initiations and have gone from the Mystery School to use that light, to turn it against the Woman and her seed.[12] They were known of old. Their hour is come.

I announce the hour that is come for the judgment of those, each and every one, who have sought to steal the light of the banner of Maitreya and the banner of the Mother. Their judgment must come to secure the way for each initiate of life.

I come for the conversion. I hold in my hand a cup of praise. One day I will bid you drink of that cup with me. It shall be unto the God that you have become. Now let us carve a path.

I Seal You in the Purple Fire

I seal you in the purple fire. I place upon you the violet-flame mantle. I see the five-pointed star. I see the golden star and I see the star of victory.

O golden light, O initiation of the five, O initiation of the six, O three times eleven, be for the ascension of the threefold flame.

Aim

Our Father, who art in heaven, that none of these may be lost is our prayer forever and forever. Amen. [18-second pause]

Come forward now that I may touch you—a blessing from my hand to your heart, that our hearts might be one. And know the infinite fire. It is the kiss of peace as two hearts leap to be as one and then to part to be a blazing sun.

The memory of the moment of the kiss of flames is forever the promise to each flame that we shall be one again. And in the preparation for that oneness, each heart shall increase, each heart shall keep the vigil of love, each heart shall know greater and greater wisdom, and each heart shall remain faithful to its First Love.*

Come now, my beloved, my firstfruits, my first chelas of ancient, oh, of ancient days. You, then, who would go before so that others might pass through the door, you who must accelerate or be placed outside the circle, you to whom it is given to redeem the ancient vow that you had somehow lost, come now. Remember your First Love. Remember your first Guru and your first Mother on earth.

[The messenger chanted the bija mantra *Aim* for approximately ten minutes as individual students came forward to receive their blessing.]

Where Is the Determination to Be the Flame?

Out of the flame of peace, I AM come. I AM come to deliver the sacred fire. Learn, then, of me. For I AM the descending fohat of the Almighty. I AM that sacred fire uniting with your own.

Learn, then, the meaning of the sacred force. When you feel the entering into your heart of that force of light, it is the requirement

---
*one's I AM Presence and twin flame

of the Law, O chela, that you meet that force with an equal force.

Thus to receive the light you must give light. If, then, when you receive that force you retreat, how easily do you retreat from the Guru?

If the Guru pushes you away, you must push again toward the Guru. You must pursue the Guru as a cosmic lover. You must be determined to have that Guru and to have no other!

You must be dauntless! Though the Mother spurns you thus, though you are turned away, you must come with a determination that will not be moved but will keep on keeping on.

If, then, the force delivered unto you is able to drive you away, you must know that it is for the strengthening, for the transmutation, for the preparation, for the bringing to the altar of a better fruit—not the bitter fruit of regret, of reticence.

Where, then, is determination? Where, then, is the determination to be the flame? For I could scarce deliver the power of my heart, for by the impact of the force, you backed away.

Thus, beloved, do you not understand? This is initiation. *This is initiation.* If you turn away when you feel the force, if you allow the force to move your determined stance to carry a light, then how can you assimilate that force?

If, perforce, the force be God and you stand fast, knowing that neither heaven nor earth would turn you from that flame, then you will be burned by that flame but you will also *become* that flame.

Now, with that power in your being, know that the world will also come with its force—God-force misqualified—and the world will also be the guru of your initiation. And you must stand also immovable, also immovable gainst that force, determined that when that energy comes upon your heart, you will meet it with the light, an equal force, a greater force, and perforce transmute, absorb, assimilate, *seize* that energy, *ride* that bull, *make* it your own whirling sphere of light that you now hurl!

Allow No One to Turn You from the Path

Beloved ones, the lesson is this: Allow no one to turn you away from the Path. Allow no one to alter your will to come to the altar and stand before the living God. Allow no one to turn you from the Path, not even the force of the Guru.

Be relentless. Do not take no for an answer but take more and more and more initiation until the force of the Guru, the force of the chela be one flame sustained—sustained from Alpha to Omega, from the Word unto the Word.

Transmute the in-between words! *Be* the Word! Therefore wherever you are, I AM that Word! And therefore the Guru and the chela are one.

I AM the source of light. I AM the source of light. I AM that source. I send you forth by that force to test the resilience of consciousness to return to the origin of the force.

Aim

March 24, 1979
Camelot
Los Angeles County, California

*I AM Maitreya.
I bring peace, peace, peace, peace
in the heart of the chela,
peace as the mighty flame,
all-consuming—consuming all unrest,
disquietude, anxiety.*

CHAPTER 9

A Meditation on the Glorious Mission of Our Brotherhood

Hail to the light! I AM come in the flame of the Ancient of Days.

I bring you greetings from my retreat in India.[1] Lo, I AM Maitreya, bearing the banner of bright love from the very heart of Sanat Kumara.

I bow before the Lord of the World. I bow before the eternal Mother. I AM in the golden pink glow-ray of your heart's glory. I AM in the sublime realization of the oneness of the master and the disciple, who together sing the song, "Drink me while I am drinking thee."[2]

O my beloved hearts, we are here. Himalaya[3] and I have come in this hour with Babaji,[4] holding a flame of the ascended and unascended masters, of the Cosmic Christs, and of the blessed Manus of earth's root races.[5] I take this opportunity to bow before the Christ Child, to pay homage unto his glory, and to wish you one and all a most joyous Noel.

The rejoicing of the hearts of the World Teachers is mine to convey to you as they anticipate this cosmic interchange announced by beloved Chananda.[6] We see the precious little children of America, of India. We see the lifewave, whom we have adored. We see the incoming lights. We see the Buddhas, the Holy Christ children.

We see those of the ten thousand avatars who have taken incarnation and the one who shall come.

In the sacred fire of the message that I bear, I bring you tidings of goodwill. I bring to you the wisdom flame of holy angels and of bodhisattvas and of those numberless numbers of white-robed saints who are the devotees of the Mother out of the retreats of India.

Choruses of jubilant pilgrims welcome you, my beloved, to the land of India. They hail your coming as a new day and a new era, and there is much excitement and activity in Darjeeling as preparations for the Mother's coming are under way.[7]

Joyous is the flame of the Brotherhood, and we would raise up our devotees worldwide into a new consciousness and a new service for the reintegration of all children of the light with the original seed of Alpha, Omega, Sanat Kumara.

The Meditation of the Buddhas

Lo, I have come. Lo, I AM here. In the name of Gautama, I bear a portion of the ruby ray. I meditate upon the ruby rose and upon the flower of your heart unfolding.

Maitreya has come to Camelot to meditate with the Mother and her sons and daughters, and so I place myself opposite the messenger, in the chair reserved for the ascended messenger.[8] By his leave I place myself there in meditation until the last word shall have been spoken on January 1, 1980.[9]

My meditation is upon the glorious divine plan and the fulfillment of the mission of our Brotherhood in these two lands [America and India] and from these focal points unto the capitals of the nations, where our forerunner, the blessed and most noble Saint Germain, has placed his freedom flame.

Around that banner of freedom there are souls gathering, souls responding. Thus, from every nation they must come ere the prophecy is fulfilled of those who are to receive the Everlasting Gospel.[10] And so I shall meditate upon every star-fire heart the world around who shall enter the light ere the century has struck its closing bells, chiming the ending and the beginning.

Here I shall be. And I invite you to meditate with me upon the golden pink glow-ray of the Lord Christ and the Lord Buddha. For the cosmic interchange of these avatars East and West is of the body and blood of the Lord, as the gold and the pink light.

They have asked me (and I am so privileged to figure in their configuration of the eighth ray[11]) to be then at the nexus of their planetary meditation, my beloved. And so we three shall pay homage unto the Ancient of Days as we also celebrate the hosts of the LORD from far-off worlds, who even now are processioning toward earth, bearing their light and their path of initiation of the eighth ray.

The Opening of the Seventh Seal

And so Lord Sanat Kumara has sealed his book on the opening of the seven-sealed book,[12] ready and waiting for the entire decade and the children of the light to open his book and to let his book be the open book again to the book of life.

Oh, how precious are his words. We bow before him as he delivers to the messenger his great truth for the liberation of every soul upon this earth through the hearts of the nearest and dearest chelas. He has reserved that light for those who have chosen to walk with the Mother in the supreme year of testing, 1979.

Many were called in the previous decades to come forth and to be prepared in this hour for this supreme delivery of the messengers' mission. Precious hearts, some tarried and could not endure, for the cares of life compelled them into other activities. Some did not care enough. Some who would become attached to the person of the messenger in idolatry would thereby find it necessary to ultimately destroy their self-created idol lest it destroy them—and all of this the illusion of their own dweller-on-the-threshold.[13]

We wish the best to all who have taken their own paths. We pray that God's gift of free will might bring them to another opportunity to serve our Brotherhood. *Therefore, we send light. Therefore, we send light. Therefore, we send light.*

Himalaya's Blessing of the Root Races

Himalaya now blesses the root races of the earth, the fourth and the fifth.[14] [12-second pause]

He blesses the angels who have embodied to serve among them. He raises the Mother light within them and prepares their temples to receive the Mother:

O blessed teaching, O blessed dharma,
  thy light is the light of all worlds.
O blessed Brotherhood of the Himalayas,
  we have come, the Mother and I.
We stand with you to challenge the false hierarchy
  of the Himalayan Brotherhood.
We come to invoke the sacred passion of the Lord.
We send our messenger
  for the pronouncement of the judgment
  upon all who have held back thy mighty light.

O Himalayan Brotherhood, O souls of light of India,
  we send forth the edict
  for the binding of the false gurus
  who have gone forth into embodiment
  into the land of Afra,[15]

who have crossed the seas to sell their wares
  to unwary chelas and would-be chelas.
O holy ones of the Himalayas,
  we come with the opening
  of the mighty stream of the Mother light
  for the cleansing and the purging.
O mighty flow of the Ganges,
  flow now the world around.
Let thy tributaries of Mother light
  be the clear crystal waters
  cleansing earth and her evolutions.
Lo, I AM here for the deliverance
  of the sons and daughters of the Mother.
Lo, the Mother is coming home, home to India—
  no longer to roam from the light
  of the Holy of Holies.

We have awaited thy coming, blessed Mother,
  for thousands upon thousands of years.
Many have come in thy name to keep thy flame.
O blessed Mother, come home.
Bring thy children,
  bring thy children to our arms of light.
We welcome thee. We welcome thee, one and all. Come home.
Blessed hearts of freedom, our prayers rise
  to the altar of blessed Omega.
Universal Mother light, piercing Mother light,
  Maha Kali, all devotees of earth bow before thy light.
Maha Kali, come, then. Sweep now into Camelot.
Place thy arms of loving light around each child
  and child-man.

O Mother of the World, O Mother of the universes,
  O Isis unveiled, O cosmic Mother,
  now let thy light swallow up the dark.
Let it be dissolved by the fohatic key that I AM, that thou art.
O thy blessed hand, O thy blessed heart,
  through thee we now impart a sacred fire,
  and the demons of the night are swallowed up.
Where the fire goes forth and trembles the earth,
  so in that fire is no time, neither is there space.
Therefore, where the fire is, evil is not,
  and the identification of evil is no more.
I send the fire of the Mother into Terra
  for the checking of destructivity.
Checkmate!

The Mother Receives Her Own

Hearts of fire, see it flow. See it glow. The fohatic key of the Mother is for the protection of her children. Lo, we are one. Lo, we have come. And the Mother and the Maitreya and the magnificent brothers and sisters of the ruby ray, bearing each one the ruby rose, come to comfort, come to bring the light of the Maha Chohan.

Aim Aim
They shall not pass!
They shall not pass!
They shall not pass!
They shall not pass!
They shall not pass!
They shall not pass!
They shall not pass! [23-second pause]

The Sound of the Om unto Infinity

Babaji summons his devotees unto light. He declares and he directs all devotees of his flame and of his path to the altar of the universal Mother.

Om Mata   Om Mata

And the Mother receives her own. By her flame they atone for every sin and sinful sense that they have entertained in her absence.

Om Mata   Om Mata

Rings of light ripple from the epicenter of my heart's meditation and from the heart of the Mother. Concentric rings of light, rippling out, form the interconnecting figure eight in the inner sanctuary. And all within this forcefield receive now these light emanations of our figure-eight manifestation, which shall be sustained unto the fulfillment of an action of the light sent from the far-off worlds by the heart of the Ancient of Days.

Ommmmmmmmmmmmmmm

The universal light knows no bounds. It carries the sound of the Om unto infinity. And with the sound of my intonation the rings of light rippling across a universe carry now the vibrational tone of the souls gathered here in order that that tone might vibrate in consonance with its corresponding cosmic tone.

And therefore the sound that is heard is of the flow of the figure eight. From the sound of the tone of the soul unto the sounding of the tone of the mighty Spirit of the I AM of each one, chords of light announce to the universe that your soul is at Camelot for the celebration of the decade of reintegration by the path of the ruby ray, the eighth ray, and the seven rays that have gone before.

[The master chants.]

I have sent forth the compressed sound of all of these chords of light into the single sound of this body of God in the earth.

Lo, I AM the Maitreya and the Guru Ma in the nucleus of the atom of lightbearers sealed in the heart of Saint Germain, of violet flame, Zadkiel, Amethyst, Holy One from the Sun, Arcturus, Victoria in light, Kuan Yin.[16]

[The master chants.]

From the God Star light of Sirius, Surya and Cuzco send forth the initiation of the light of the interaction of the white sphere unto the blue sphere.[17]

Ommmmmmmmmmmmmmm

I AM Maitreya. I bring *peace, peace, peace, peace* in the heart of the chela, *peace* as the mighty flame, all-consuming—consuming all unrest, disquietude, anxiety.

Ommmmmmmmmmmmmm
Vaivasvata Manu   Vaivasvata Manu
Him Himalaya Manu

[48-second pause]

We seal the community of the brethren. We seal the community of light worldwide. We seal the hearts in the flame of Maitreya and in the flame of the Guru Ma.

O blessed light of community, light invincible, light that is love, shine on! Shine on! For thy dispensation is come.

Ommmmmmmmmmmmmmm

Peace be unto you, our most beloved.

December 29, 1979
Camelot
Los Angeles County, California

*Your own Great God Self
is like unto the secret love star.
It is a secret until you have truly climbed
the starbeams back to the Source,
there to discover the mystery of the ages.
And the secret is no secret anymore.*

CHAPTER 10

Love of the Person and the Law of the Word: God and My Right

The Ritual of the Great Interchange

O light from the heart of central suns of far-off worlds, light of Manus, light of freedom's banner now within the heart of devotee unfurled, I, Maitreya, come in the ritual of the great interchange.

There is a sphere of light within my own soul that represents the path of my chelaship under the Lord Sanat Kumara. Hand in hand, Gautama and I would go through meadow and forests, climbing to the heights of the Himalayas—not in search but in surrender unto the eternal Guru, the everlasting star, that light whom we knew as the very Person of heartbeat.

We would follow the beating of our hearts to its logical conclusion in the heart of the Ancient of Days, where so many devotees have found succor and a flame and the place of rest in preparation for going out once again on the path of initiation—that is, initiation according to this world and all that it contains, even the crosscurrents of lifestreams and races and fallen ones and types of personalities that are the antithesis of the Godhead.

Thus the way of soul elevation upon earth includes this path of soul testing by the very presence of the rebellious ones, and it provides the initiatic stream of our Brotherhood emanating from Sirius, from the retreats of the Himalayas and the etheric citadels of the Brotherhood.

Therefore, beloved hearts, there is a path of initiation that is reflective of your own individual attainment of light, regardless of this world or the next or wherever you may abide. This path of initiation has to do with light—the alchemy of light, the equation of light, the mathematical formula of light, and all that you contain in discipline, order, harmony, wisdom, and, most of all, intense love for the Source.

Your own Great God Self is like unto the secret love star. It is a secret until you have truly climbed the starbeams back to the Source, there to discover the mystery of the ages. And the secret is no secret anymore.

The Inner Path of the Ascension

Hearts afire with the love of God, this inner path, spiraling up, up the ladder of the five secret rays, carries you to the very center and to the pinnacle of the I AM Presence. The initiation of outer worlds demands that those who climb to the star of the mighty I AM Presence descend once again to release that light—in measured cadence and according to the calculus of the Spirit—for the judgment, for the sacred fire, for the rolling back and the stripping of the fallen ones of their misuse of the sacred fire.

Thus there are terms and conditions of servitude within the Great White Brotherhood upon earth. These differ from those of other planetary homes. But nevertheless, the science of the Spirit from within, the science of the inner attainment, is the same. And therefore there are classes in the retreat of Serapis Bey and the seraphim, where students gather from many systems to learn of the inner path of the ascension.

There are other classes where students also gather from this system and beyond to learn of the particular circumstances that require an astute and an intensely compassionate application of the law of grace. Some individuals who attend these classes from other parts of the systemic worlds, here to study the condition of earth, from time to time take incarnation to experience in a more direct manner the testings of life in the outer conditions of the nations of earth.

The Door of Heaven's Gate Is Open

Now then, you have assembled at this quarter of Summit University—truly a university of the Spirit sponsored by the Great White Brotherhood—to sit at the feet of the Goddess of Justice.[1] Therefore I, Maitreya, consider it just that you ought to realize that some among you have embodied from out of the classrooms of Serapis Bey to study and to master the conditions of earth so that you could return to other planetary homes where there are also dire conditions in this leg of the Kali Yuga, this very dark cycle of returning karma.

Some who have attended these classes have now been upon earth a second, a third, even a fourth incarnation. For as it happens, pitifully and sorrowfully, some forget the mission, the nature of the encounter, and they become all too attached or embroiled in the conditions of earth. Thereby making karma, they press on in another and another embodiment.

Blessed hearts, I have stood before Serapis Bey. I have stood before the Lords of Karma to sponsor you, that you might disentangle yourselves from this evolution, gain the mastery, and (now that you have spent some time here) also accelerate the inner walk with God and thereby insure—through the balancing of karma, the use of the violet flame, and the certain knowledge of the path of the ascension—that in returning to finish that unfinished business on other planetary homes, you might be assured that the door of heaven's gate is open and that you also might ascend after a concluding and glorious, victorious incarnation for the fulfillment of that cycle.

Now, this is a most unusual circumstance at Summit University, and it has occurred because I have made a study of certain lifestreams upon the planetary body and I have determined that there are deserving souls who have become embroiled and enmeshed in the conditions of earth.

Considering the maya and the bombardment of the senses from the hour of birth and beyond, this is understandable. And yet I must say, in all defense of the Karmic Board and the ascended masters, that all who have sojourned with earth for these various purposes have come well trained and aware, but little by little they have been enticed away from the straight and narrow path of cosmic purpose.

Thus these circumstances and others, which have caused to be assembled at Summit University this group of lifestreams, have to do with the light, most intense, of the heart of beloved Portia herself* and her own desire to transfer to you a living flame that you might bear into the midst of a crowded world, which often seems most lonely.

Perfect Love Casts Out the Entire Sphere of Human Creation

Dear hearts afire with love, I would part the veil. I would open the way so that you might touch the hem of the garment of

---
*See endnote 1.

Kuthumi, of the Lord Christ Jesus, and others. I would even accelerate the light now, that you might have imparted to you a fragrance of the auric emanation of your own twin flame.

It is our desire to enable you to feel a greater proximity to the elder brothers and sisters who are indeed just beyond the veil. We are so very near. And the warmth of our love would caress you if your attunement were not so much with the world and its absence of that love.

Our desire is that you seek in God, your own mighty I AM Presence, the solace for human grief and every human need. For thereby you could, if you would, in short order dissolve some of those binding conditions that cause you to feel enslaved and that truly tear from you the heights of God's own consummate love.

Thus I commend you to the heart of the Buddha even as I stand before you. For I draw close to you, even to your very midst, and I accelerate the interchange whereby you now receive the sphere of light that contains the record of my own discipleship with Gautama under the Lord Sanat Kumara.

For as I have pondered the sweet mystery of life, which is the chela in the heart of the Guru and the Guru in the heart of the chela, I have desired that you should know truly what is the path of life whereby you put on concentric rings of the aura of the Buddha, of the aura of the Mother, and begin to experience in actuality that mighty figure-eight flow of being.

O my beloved, I would draw you intensely and tenderly into my heart. For of all of the words that have passed through your heart during these weeks together, it is the word of love, the tenderness of the Good Shepherd, and the realization of this perfect love that casts out the entire sphere of human creation, the whole ball of wax, as you might say.

Think, then, of the wax melting in the sun. Realize that those who have attempted to fly using wax to attach their wings, truly will not fly.[2] For the wax, symbolic of the maya of the ego, will always prove insufficient to the task. You cannot fly to the sun on human pride, the wax of ambition.

The Right of the Christ Self within You to Reign

Beloved hearts, it is not even lawful for you to claim "my right" but to realize that the motto of the kings, "God and my right"[3] has to do with the right of the Christ Self within you to reign. The human consciousness, imperfect, has no rights or privileges except those accorded to it by the mighty I AM Presence, even as the soul has access to the exercise of free will.

Realize, then, that your right to be and to express free will is always by grace, and this grace is afforded moment by moment by moment by the free will of the LORD God Almighty. It is not something that is yours to keep by right, but by grace. And grace is always contingent upon the state of consciousness of the individual.

Grace, as that element of the Holy Spirit, descends only to the level of a certain frequency of vibration of light and consciousness. And as long as the soul is attuned with that level, that soul is draped in the grace and the graciousness of the Person of God, of the holy office, and of the garments worn. But when there is the subtle slipping away from that office and from its vibration, so it is as the slip of the cup. And therefore there are moments when those who ought to be in the grace of Almighty God lose that grace, and it is then that they cry, "My right!" And they claim the authority that is not theirs except when they are under the shadow of their own Christ Self, who is indeed the most gracious King of kings, the Immanuel—the "God with us."[4]

The Balance of Love for the Guru with Obedience to the Law

Blessed hearts, consider then the scales of justice. For we too were initiated on the path of justice by the ascended lady masters. Consider these scales and consider the balance of the Path.

The Path contains the requirement, on the one side, of obedience unto the Law—obedience unto the Law as the Word of the Guru who embodies the Law.

Realize, then, that the requirement of the chela is not obedience to a set of blueprints or to a code of conduct or to a set of regulations and rules or commandments of life, but rather it is obedience to the spoken Word of the Gurus in the unbroken chain of the Word incarnate whereby the pronouncements of the Word have also been collected and codified.

But, beloved hearts, one must never lose sight of the fact that the Law itself, as stated, as set forth, is the manifestation of the Word. Therefore, balancing the obedience to the Law on the other side of the scale is intense love for the Teacher—intense love for the Person of God whereby one is infused with the light and thereby obedient to the Impersonal Personality[5] of the Law itself on the other side of the scale.

How easy it is to tip the balance in favor of love for the Guru! But when this is out of balance with obedience to the Law, the scales tip. And then, you see, suddenly you find yourselves rocked into a state of idolatry, where nearness to the Guru or love of the Guru replaces the work of the ages, the mighty work whereof Jesus spoke: "The Father worketh hitherto, and I work."[6]

Thus the balance of the Law is revealed as the Person, the personal and the impersonal manifestation. And if perchance you should leave off loving the Person of the Word in every ascended master as well as in the embodied avatar, then, beloved hearts, your devotion would quickly degenerate to that legalism and that humanistic assessment of the Law whereby the mechanical, rote performance is deemed sufficient.

And therefore once again the scales are tipped. For without the daily renewal in the heart of devotion and of love for the Guru, the Law itself becomes an empty shell, no longer charged with the original light and intent of the Word, the spoken Word of the one that spake it in the beginning.

If indeed the Law as a writing were sufficient, the angels would merely deposit books upon the altars of the mosques and temples and sanctuaries of life. Indeed, it would not have been necessary for the Manus to come to the planetary systems and to inaugurate the cycles of their dispensations with the pronouncement of the Word itself.

Realize then, beloved hearts, that in those eras of the Law, when the Guru is present and when the speaking of the Word and the hearing of the Word is the sole communication that is allowed, and because souls have not descended from the Christ mind, they are aware of that spoken Word and there is less departure from devotion of the Person and Impersonality of the Law. For these reside in the single light of the Initiator.

Therefore there is a concentration upon the center of the scales as the Tree of Life itself, and one enters into the unity of the Word as Person and the Law that is codified. And thus no longer twain, but the balance of life itself becomes—by the law of correspondences—you, the chela, sitting directly neath your own vine and fig tree as the mighty I AM Presence, with the intercession of the intermediary, the Christ mind itself.

Beloved hearts, there are few if any among mankind today who can sustain an untainted at-one-ment with the mighty I AM Presence without deviating from this singular balance of devotion to the Person and the impersonal Spirit of God. Therefore there is yet the need for embodied messenger, embodied Guru. Realize, therefore, that all things contain the essentials of cosmic purpose, even our gathering together here today.

The Opportunity to Accelerate in the Office of Chela

Mindful then of your heart's longing to perfect your immortal destiny, mindful then that some have reached barriers (albeit self-created), I have come to widen your capacity to experience God and life truly as these are in balance as Above, so below.

Realize that "God and my right" signify the presence of the mighty I AM Presence and the Christ Self. And never, ever was it the intent of the hierarchy to impute to the imperfected human self this ordination of authority. Rather, by grace there is the dropping of the mantle upon each individual, that that individual might enter into that office and grow in the grace of the office. How quickly some have trampled upon the mantles of their gurus. How quickly some have trampled upon their own.

Beloved hearts, I desire, in answer to your call, to give you the opportunity to accelerate in a holy office. The office of which I speak is the office of chela. Do you understand that to be a chela is to be called of God unto discipleship? One cannot claim the mantle of the chela, but one may aspire to it and serve lovingly toward that goal.

Your acceptance as a chela by a single master of the Great White Brotherhood is certainly to be desired and highly prized among those who study in our retreats. For you see, when you are received vis-à-vis the ascended master in the one-to-one relationship of the mighty figure-eight flow, it is a signal that there is trust in the heart of the master—sufficient trust to place a portion of himself within your heart and then to begin the weaving of the figure-eight action and the mighty flow of light. Your interaction with this dispensation and your adoration of the Person of the Guru will give to you a most fitting opportunity to come into alignment with your own God-free being at the behest and sponsorship of one who is God-free and ascended.

Realize the immense opportunity at hand. Realize that there must be a certain coequality twixt the Guru and the chela—even though it is the Guru whose name is spelled with a capital *G*, signifying that the greater portion of Godhood rests within the Guru, and that the chela, always spelled with a lowercase *c*, is yet in the process of putting on the skeins of light.

But, you see, even a single point of Godhood conveyed by the Guru results in a sort of balance, if you will, whereby it is God who is in polarity with God—although it is the God that has been invested into your heart, which you make your own by your soul's attunement with your very own Christ Self, your mighty I AM Presence, and the Guru himself.

Let Each One Submit to One's Own Beloved Christ Self

Now, beloved hearts, in the ceremony of this interchange I desire to place within you the sphere that contains the recordings of my chelaship. This sphere I make available entirely to your Christ Self and in its entirety.

Let each one, then, submit to the rule—by law and love, by person and by Word—to one's own beloved Christ Self. Let it be an unmitigated love. Let it be uncompromising. Let it accelerate. For by that love you will melt the successive sheaths of this sphere of light and there will pour unto you, the soul on the Path, another circle of initiation, another world of Maitreya, another layer of the mantle of the office of chela.

To occupy the office of chela is the most noble and the highest of all activities upon earth! I say this because there is yet human questioning and doubt and confusion in the hearts of some as to whether to do this or to do that. Beloved hearts, all of the education you need—in the outer sense and in all of the training—can be gained by you as a part of your direct chelaship under the ascended masters, which perforce must also be monitored and directed by the embodied messenger.

All that you need in the way of preparation for the mighty work of the ages upon this planetary body, and perhaps on other systems, can be acquired and fulfilled while you are in direct service to the Guru in embodiment, who represents the essential Mother flame of all ascended masters, thereby providing you with the link to any of our bands.

For truly, the one common light of Mother is both our source and the object of our devotion. Thus we have raised up Mother flame and Mother heart to represent a wide span of consciousness of the Great White Brotherhood in order to accommodate the many paths and evolutions and directions that are upon the varied lifewaves of this earth.

Realize, then, that the closer your proximity to the Word, the more intense your initiations. Knowing this, you must realize that even this sphere of my own chelaship will accelerate the cooking out of your subconscious of that substance that ought to, by all rights, be put into the flame.

Thus it is, you might say, a calculated dispensation—calculated to give you opportunity. But the moment that that opportunity should be misused, there is the immediate withdrawal of the sphere of my chelaship so as to cause you the least uncomfortability, karma, and proximity to the light, because once that sphere and its fiery coils surround you, it is also relentless in the pursuit of darkness, even as truth swallows up error.

And the serpent swallowing its tail must always result in a higher and higher manifestation of God's being, for the law of transcendence is fulfilled. For as the LORD God partakes of my body, of my blood, truly there is the acceleration to the next ring. For the serpent cannot swallow its tail without transformation, which comes from the assimilation of the very essence of the Holy Spirit itself. And this is a great mystery.

The Opening of the Temple Door

Let those who have ears to hear, hear what is the message of the Spirit unto the souls of light, who are the churches[7] in this hour.

My beloved, I would not have you misinformed, nor would I have you misunderstand the purpose of the first level of this university of the Spirit. We describe it as the opening of the temple door—the opening of the door of the heart, the opening of the door of the Christ Self of the individual soul. Truly it is the first step on the Path. Therefore, let it not be that some of you consider that with this amount of light and teaching you have all you need until the hour of your ascension.

It is true, as our messenger has said, that the teaching itself is a sufficiency. For behind the teaching and every word that is spoken is a great sphere of light containing infinite wisdom and the science of its application. But, beloved hearts, the mere hearing of the teaching is not the transfer of the ability to open the door to these spheres—or, as we would put it, to melt the sheaths of consciousness behind the Word.

It is following the Word and its vibration back to that very source of the Sun behind the sun of manifestation that is the Path. Therefore, let those who cherish Maitreya and the ongoing path of initiation draw close to the love of the Mother's heart and realize this opportunity to serve in many arenas of life across the planetary body and yet to serve in direct alignment with the messenger.

There is a difference, then. Some choose to go forth with a little knowledge of the Law and to become a law unto themselves. The serpents have taught this. They have encouraged the proud to take what is given and to go forth to become greater than the instrument of the Law, to discard the instrument and to think that with a little getting they will indeed conquer.

These have erred and taken upon themselves an immense karma for the letting down of lifestreams who ought to have been connected or reconnected to the original fount instead of left to depend upon those who have not occupied the holy office of chela and therefore have not had the Spirit of the Word or the instrumentation to convey that Spirit.

The Tendency of the Human Mind to Play the Game of Guru

The messenger has told you of the event of suicide and warned of this very circumstance. To be cleansed is one thing, but the requirement to "Go, and sin no more"[8] must be held to as joyously as the original desire to be made whole.

Thus, beloved hearts, let it not be said that those who have sat with Maitreya, with Portia and Saint Germain and others of our bands, should go out and then play the "game of guru," considering how much wiser they are than those unschooled in the mystery school of the Brotherhood.

I must expose to you thoroughly the tendency and the penchant of the human mind to do just that. And I must reveal to you this temptation and also counsel you that truly you have only entered into the beginning of the Law.

The pursuit of the path of service will unfold for you petals of the Mother's heart, which cannot be wrested, which cannot be discovered, which cannot be taken but only acquired by blessed assimilation through that closeness and oneness of love that is never idolatry but always the love of the greater and greater light shining just beyond the veil.

Indeed, You Are Learning at Inner Levels

O beloved hearts, let your love indeed go to the Mother, but let it pass through. For she is also an open door to octaves fair. Let it pass through swiftly, contacting succeeding chains of hierarchy.

I long for you to behold, in some moments of teaching, how being upon being of light, tier upon tier of angels as frequencies accelerate, overshadow the release. And there is an acceleration of the person of the Teacher until you could behold the fullness and the glory of her own ascended master light body in octaves fair, where etheric retreats and students of the light receive the very same message by the frequency of the Word of the I AM Presence.

No wonder some of you recall inner retreat experiences, sitting at the feet of the messengers and learning those lessons of life that perhaps your ears could not hear in this level of densification. Indeed, you are learning at inner levels. Indeed, your higher bodies are participating. Indeed, your souls come and go to the inner retreats. This is why it is called a university of the Spirit!

Beloved hearts, this term has naught to do with the world's conception of a university according the degrees of this world. You have not heard of degrees being awarded, for there are none that can be given. For the degrees are of the Spirit and spiritual, and they are worn with great honor as you receive them at inner levels.

And you know, as I know. And one day your entire consciousness will have that awareness that you have indeed accelerated. And in the hour of your ascension you will have gained, so to speak, golden bars of merit that have not been won by many other lifestreams, even saints who have ascended, because they did not have the opportunity to be a part of my own Mystery School and to receive the direct initiations by the spoken Word from one in physical embodiment. For it is only by this method that we are able to curb the tendencies of the serpent mind, that we are able to encourage and to correct a certain wobbling in the four lower bodies that occurs when there is even the slightest vibration of being out of alignment.

The Rebuke Is Always Rooted in the Inner Vibration

Our messenger is sensitized and most sensitive to our vibration, and therefore the rebuke for outer conditions is always rooted in the rebuke of inner vibration [of the chela]—the intangible, that *something* that must be dissolved even as it has crystallized in the astral or mental body—in order for you to penetrate higher octaves and higher vibrations.

This is an ongoing process, day by day. And this is why we have applauded and assisted El Morya in the extension and outreach of this organization in order to provide chelas with this opportunity to serve, in a world sense, and to accelerate in the course of service by having that supervision that is so necessary in order to point out the unwindings of the human consciousness as these come forth in the course of service itself.

Life must be outplayed—the great superconscious Being, the Monad[9] of life, as well as the subconscious—and it is the outplaying of these spirals, beloved, that enables you to view the passing scenes of reality and unreality.

The Key to Objectivity on the Path

I give you then, my hearts, the key to objectivity on the Path. This key is in my person and in my own path, which by the grace of the universal Christ I made my own, and by that grace alone.

For I know well what is humility, and I can tell you, beloved hearts, that humility comes when you sit at the feet of Sanat Kumara. Humility comes when you hear his heartbeat within the chamber of your own heart, and then you hear his heartbeat as the great magnet of Almighty God magnetizing your own heart. And then, lo, you hear the moment when your heartbeat and his own are one and there is only the one beat in unison of life, as Above, so below. Beloved hearts, that humility comes when you feel yourself enfolded by the mystical love of Sanat Kumara.

These gifts of God are to be cherished more than all else. These gifts of God, my beloved, come by the soul's inner penetration and interpenetration with the fiery coils of the Initiator. Let those who do not consider themselves prepared for interaction with the sphere of my chelaship merely give me the sign of their decline and I will graciously withhold it until another cycle of turning when you are ready.

Beloved hearts, readiness for confrontation with any part of God is certainly a most serious science of the soul. It is a part of the seraphic science. For the seraphim themselves are the great confronters of man's identity and of his soul. Mighty seraphs welcome the opportunity to confront the soul of light on the path of life.

I Send a Single Ray of Hope to Every Heart on Earth

Blessed hearts, remember love. My love impels me to give you all that the Great Law will allow. My love impels me to understand the present plight of your soul, the dilemma of your inner being in contradistinction to the outer manifestation, even the dilemma of your karma.

But I AM Maitreya. Each and every one of you knows me well. You know my face, my footprint, my vibration. You have heard my comings and my goings in the inner temples of the Spirit.

10 • Love of the Person and the Law of the Word: God and My Right

I say, then, this is a most august occasion. For it is an hour out of a cosmic cycle when I may sit with you as we have not sat together in this group for many an aeon. It is an hour when there might pass between us the secrets of the heart, confessions, and affirmations of good. It is an hour when I may be myself with those students who have dutifully and, in most cases, lovingly prepared themselves for my coming.

I send a single ray of hope to every heart on earth that is affiliated with the heart of this messenger by devotion to the flame of life. I send forth a ray of hope for progress on the Path, for increasing God Self-awareness.

I send hope now to those who have not tied themselves to the Great White Brotherhood. And through my aura, the Great White Brotherhood extends its outreach into the earth—gathering, gathering unto itself those whose hands reach out to touch our garment but who cannot quite reach. Thus I extend the rope of hope. And the hand may grasp it and *hold,* then, that which is real, that which will not steal from them their own Self-consciousness in God.

O dear hearts, how we long to see upliftment and a ceasing of all struggle and a healing of the wounds of the nations and to see understanding replace misunderstanding.

Hearts of light, come into my own.

[24-second pause]

The Snowy White Bird in the Golden Cage

There is a little bird, snowy white, in a little golden cage in my heart chamber. He sings a song of love and the song of the homing.

This little white bird is not imprisoned but entered the cage voluntarily and shut the door, desiring to be an adornment at the altar where the chela may come to meditate—the chela whom

I have chosen, not who has chosen me. This snowy white bird sings the song, the love song of twin flames. And do you know, he sings the song, *the keynote of each one's I AM Presence* as that chela approaches the altar of initiation in my heart.

Most blessed outcropping of the Holy Spirit, most blessed being of light, this little bird understands the mystery of chelaship and would illustrate the happiness of the soul to be in the birdcage yet totally free to fly to the heart of the I AM Presence of anyone, even from here to the Central Sun, to meditate upon the keynote, to learn it and to sing it in adoration of that Monad of light and of that soul becoming the Monad.

When therefore you meditate in this hour, here in the sanctuary of the Holy Grail, I ask that you visualize the snowy white bird in the golden cage as you hear him sing the song of love of your own God Presence I AM.

Let this little bird teach you the mystery of perfect love and perfect service, and, my beloved, perfect freedom within the disciplined environment of a cosmic grid. You see, whether that grid be planet Earth or another world or the sea or the sky or the earth or your favorite place or your most unfavorite place—Camelot or the cities of the nations, Serapis Bey's retreat or your own untransmuted human creation—that cosmic grid represents your opportunity for service unto victory.

Contemplate the little bird and then determine whether it is "God and my right" as your own private interpretation of the Word, or "God and my right" as your own mighty I AM Presence and Christ Self that will become the leading authority in your life, the leading authority as the mighty lifestream that not only connects you to the Great God Star but pulls you in, year by year, as you, the soul, are the anchor, and God himself is the great mother ship.

Move through the Sea by the Light of the Stars

O hearts of light, indeed you are anchor points—under the sea of the astral plane and in the heart of the earth—of the great, great light of the mother ship of our Brotherhood. So it is that the clipper ship is my symbol and the symbol of your soul's journey in time and in space.

There are no coordinates in the sea itself. Thus the ancient mariner charts by the polar magnet, the North Star, and other heavenly bodies. Thus when charting your course, beloved hearts of light, you must realize that it is not the corks bobbing on the sea that can ever be the coordinates of your journey—uncompleted spirals and imperfected ones. Rather, move through the sea by the light of the stars. Remember Maitreya and remember that the way is clear and the starlight is like crystal. And when there is confusion or illusion, it can certainly be consumed by the violet flame and by the pure in heart.

Let those who would know Portia and Saint Germain now undertake the self-disciplining of the soul that leads only to the Divine Whole of love and love and love.

In the fullness of the joy of opportunity, I commend you unto the Guru and the Law.

December 4, 1980
Camelot
Los Angeles County, California

*Rest in absolute peace
within the heart at regular intervals.
Learn by the discipline of the mind
to go within, swiftly!
Learn to hurl the strength of your mind
to the eye of God, to the heart
of your I AM Presence.*

CHAPTER 11

The Dilemma of the Soul in the Evolutionary Cosmos

From out the heart of love, I come. My love is a concern for your very soul, for the perfecting of your path, and for your awareness of those reaches of the mind of God that are just beyond your present awareness.

How can one sense what one knows not, when one knows it not?

How can one sense one's need to push back the barriers of the mind or sheaths of consciousness outworn?

How can one know the way to go when one does not perceive the need to go any way?

Our Lord Gautama and Sanat Kumara before him, and so on in the vast hierarchical chain, each in his own way has considered this dilemma of the soul that is in the evolutionary cosmos. The answer that has come forth is the eternal chain of hierarchy.

If you do not know that sensitivity that you ought to have but you do not, I can assure you that the one who is above you in the chain of hierarchy knows it. Therefore, listen to that one! Follow that one! Acknowledge that one as teacher, even if it be but in a single field of human endeavor.

Those who think they know it all—and, oddly enough, there are many on this ship of fools called planet Earth—end up knowing nothing. For they know less and less, not perceiving that which they know not.

Thus, the obvious conclusion is that without the Guru, one recedes. There is no maintaining even of one's present position. For what is "present position"? There is none, since life is the law of self-transcendence, ever unfolding in the law of cycles.

Therefore, you see, if you are expected to be something in a moment from now that now you are not—because the law of cycles governs all—how will you move with that spiral if you cannot take the hem of another's garment and follow or be swept up in the draft of that one's attainment? This is a predicament that is upon mankind and they know it not! For the very lesson I teach is already beyond their present awareness.

The Great Divine Director has addressed himself to this dilemma, and he has spoken of it to you in this hall. I come to give you an understanding of why the bodhisattvas have chosen to be bodhisattvas, tarrying with an evolution blinded and increasingly blinded by its own blindness.

The Chain of Hierarchy

Blessed hearts, you can see the condition of a planet as we see it. You understand that instead of moving forward, the products of the educational systems of this nation have less and less capacity to express the Word—as language skills, as mathematics, or as other subjects. Consequently, standards are lowered. The tests become easier and easier, as educators (who ought not to have the name) are not willing to face the fact that they are failing in the transfer of the light of the heart, which is the only true illumination of any soul.

Without the flow of love-wisdom of Helios and Vesta through

the teacher, the pupil will not mount a spiral, for the spiral is nonexistent. And if the teacher be not a part of the chain of hierarchy, then that teacher cannot attach his pupils to the chain to which he himself is not attached! Therefore, the bodhisattvas—maintaining the flame of hierarchy in the many dimensions and planes of consciousness—have come, placing themselves very near to those whom they would push up the ladder of life.

Oh, you thought you were being *pulled!* Well, blessed hearts, we are beneath you, *pushing you up*—for the very simple reason that some do not even know the way that is up from the way that is down, simply because they have lost the inner compass of life.

Some think heaven to be hell, and hell, heaven! There are those who enjoy being in the astral realm and would be most uncomfortable in the etheric plane. Why, there are those who are not even comfortable to be seated next to one of you! Have you ever noted how they have moved themselves from your side in public places? Blessed hearts, do not take it personally. [Laughter] It is their demons who cannot get along with your angels! [Laughter] Since the angels are most fearsome to the demons, it is they who move. But sometimes you also remove yourselves from those places where your soul would imbibe an unhealthy atmosphere. And so it is wise.

A Love That Is Pure and Perfect

Well, then, Serapis has come to apprise you of a love that is pure and perfect[1]—of a spiral that is now released of a ruby ray that you will only come to understand on the battlefield of life.

How can we explain and explain again? We do our best. We send you out. We let world karma do the rest. And you come back all the wiser for your experiencing of the Path.

There is no substitute for experience. There is no substitute for the teacher who can interpret experience for you and therefore give you the eyes to see—seeing through the veils of maya, seeing through the illusion, the smoke screen of the fallen ones.

Some have said that they never understood what is in the daily newspaper until they heard the word of Mother's manifestos or the messengers' releases for many years.[2] Some have said that they had never understood Light and Darkness or the conspiracy[3] or the path of initiation. Thus, you see, the Word has a way of communicating itself to you, despite the discrepancy between the teacher and the pupil. This is a miracle on the face of it! When you come to think of it, it is a result of interpenetration of magnetic fields and electromagnetic currents. It is a meshing of teacher and pupil.

There are some who will never be convinced that the Shroud of Turin is the image of the Lord Christ! These so-called scientists are filled with doubt. They are like water bags of doubt. When punctured, it would all come out and they would be no more. For their total identity is doubt, more doubt, and self-doubt! And then they make their pronouncements of doubt as though they were the empirical method of science itself.

Well, beloved hearts, there are some who can never see beyond or *feel* beyond the physical person, whether of the messenger, whether of a loved one, whether of anything from a blade of grass to a star.

How can you expect them to mesh with the Word or to desire the Guru, who obviously is taking you into spirals passing through your own nonphysical matrix leading to universes of light that are still a part of your very own being?

Thus, those who assemble to hear our Word are those not content with the physical grid of life that they use to navigate in the physical octave. They are probers of the mysteries of the octaves Above and below and through the sound ray to the soundless sound.

Testing the Teaching, Challenging, and Then Proving the Law

The hierarchy of light, the Buddhas, bodhisattvas, and masters of the wisdom ray are pleased with the expanded capacity of the mind of Christ within the chelas of the Great White Brotherhood that has occurred in this fourteen-month cycle.[4] We see that you are wiser for our teaching, wiser for your experiences in testing the teaching, challenging, and then proving the Law—as the Law will prove itself to you, as the Law will never be offended if you challenge it and say, "Show me, Lord! I believe. Help thou mine unbelief! Show me the proof of thy Word."

When you ask for proof, be not surprised how it comes. Come it will! And if you are objective and free, nonprejudiced, you will have to go where proof leads you. But if you are narrow-minded and bigoted and close your eyes to blatant reality, fearing what will be required of you and your compromise of life, then, blessed hearts, beware. For the karma of closing your eyes to the proof of truth standing before you is spiritual blindness followed by physical blindness in this or a succeeding incarnation.

Karma is instantaneous. Take care, then. Be honest in your interaction with the ascended masters and we will be honest with you. Above all, do not trifle with the Great Law. Do not play with fire, as your mothers have already taught you. The same rules apply, yet we are in ongoing dimensions of life.

The Oncoming Dark Cycle and the Misuses of Power on This Planet

Thus, I come as I concern myself with your awareness of the oncoming Dark Cycle that will begin April 23.[5] Entering the hierarchy of the initiations of Capricorn, planet Earth and her evolutions will receive the return of their misqualified energies, misqualifying the light of the Person of the Father, of his principle, his power, his omnipresence—indeed, the misuses of the all-power of God.

Here in the Person of the Father, here in the Presence of Alpha, who has come to grace the earth,[6] is the presence of all-power in heaven and earth. It is this light of Alpha and Alpha's current that has been misqualified. Inasmuch as it is absolute power, absolute God in manifestation as Brahma, you will be dealing with the perversion of the Absolute as the presence of absolute Evil personified in the anti-God manifestations of the Nephilim,[7] their mechanization man,[8] their Cain civilization, and all that has been built upon this planetary body in the successive spirals going back for millions of years.

It will be a year for serious consideration. It will be a year when your tie to the God Star, Sirius[9] will be of utmost importance. For the momentum of the God Star, Sirius is the very balance of all misuses of the light of God the Father on planet Earth and in this system of worlds.

The misuses of power on this planet by the Nephilim are connected with their misuses of power on other planets and systems. Therefore, opening the pandora's box of this cycle of karma leads to other boxes, and they are as interconnected as interconnecting computers of the fallen ones. They are as interconnected as the connectedness of all life in the Spirit of the Great White Brotherhood.

I urge you to tarry at Camelot in the morning, to assemble to decree for the sealing of the Inner Retreat[10] and all that concerns it. This we desire to see completed before the mounting momentum of the next Dark Cycle takes hold.

You have already been warned of and have experienced the lashback of the dragon's tail under the hierarchy of Sagittarius.

Do not underestimate it in these final hours before the turning of the cosmic clock![11] There is, as well, the overlapping into the new cycle of the past cycle. Thus, there will be experienced (as there is now) the overlapping of the revenge of the fallen ones as they move with their momentum of the judgment of the children of the light—the mouthings of the accuser of the brethren, their constant criticism, and the mode of their mind whereby whatever they look upon that is of the light they automatically condemn.

They are computerized to condemnation! Thus, wherever the spring flowers peep through as the budding consciousness of the chela, at subconscious planetary levels there is the put-down of that burst of joy and freedom and light.

You will notice that often when you express your joy midst people—ordinary people, neither good nor evil—they will somehow disfigure that joy, discolor it, dampen it, and you go away feeling less joyous for having expressed your joy. Such is the carnal mind. Such is the mark of the presence of the Nephilim consciousness on planet Earth that affects many, though they be not of it.

The Office of Christ Is the Judgment of Antichrist

Blessed hearts, the release of Alpha to you is stupendous. We must not underestimate the going forth of his light or the intense rejection of that light. Such light incites the very anger that originally produced the arrogance of the fallen ones, who seized heaven by force in their perversion of the absolute power of the Almighty One.

You are Christed ones, and the office of Christ is the judgment of Antichrist. Let us *put* it there! Let us *stand* there! Let us *seal* it there! Let the judgment *descend* ere their judgment come as point/counterpoint.

The Dark Cycle is not the only cycle released! There is always the light cycle in each year. The original momentum of attainment of all evolutions of this planetary body under the hierarchy of Capricorn, out of the great causal body of the Great Divine Director, can be invoked by you daily [through the science of the spoken Word] as the antidote to the daily return of mankind's karma. Use it! There are millions of cosmic beings who have won, who have graduated from this system of worlds. All of their God-good, all of their light, is accessible!

Therefore, the key in the arch is the call. Without the call you enter into the spirals of the shrinking-man syndrome, of which the Great Divine Director has spoken. If you do not expand hour by hour, you shrink. I wink as I say this, and I trust that in the wink you will not be shorter than you were before. [Laughter]

Pace Yourselves as Runners in the Race

Do you see, blessed hearts? I counsel you on the upward way. We are mountain climbers all! Our exercise in running is uphill. Then when we are on level ground, we are at ease and well trained.

It is the upward spiral. It does require striving. But there is rest and there is rhythm to life. You are not machines. You must discover the law of the seven and the seven steps[12] to the precipitation of the flame of your own God-mastery. If you do not observe them, you will find that though you think you are striving, you may have reached a plateau and are entering into levels of mediocrity that you know not. The full capacity of your God flame and your continuing in this segment of the spiral of the victory of earth depends upon your pacing of yourselves as runners in the race.

The law of the rest is the law of the relief, even in music. Take a lesson from the music of the spheres. Rest in absolute peace within the heart at regular intervals. Learn by the discipline of the mind to go within, swiftly! Learn to hurl the strength of your mind to the eye of God, to the heart of your I AM Presence, to make instantaneous contact and to discover the rest in motion that is the mark of Mercurians and Maitreyans, which I trust you shall all be very soon.

The race is to the swift and the strong, and they have a science to their swiftness and their strength. Learn it! Watch them! "Watch me. I can fly!" Blessed hearts, think how long the ascended masters have been going. They do not chart their course by a mere embodiment but by golden cycles—golden cycles of life.

Perfect Love Is the Way to Raise Up Perfect Wisdom

Let us take first things first. The hour approaches and the New Day is at hand. Let us seal the Inner Retreat by our love! Let us seal this conference by not neglecting this most necessary and most sacred of the Brotherhood's endeavor. Let us look alert, and with courage greet the oncoming cycles.

In past ages it has been the return karma of mankind's misuse of the light in some cycle of Capricorn or Cancer that has triggered cataclysm. Let us pray that this cataclysm be neither personal nor planetary but that your liberal use of the violet flame will provide oil in the gears of life and cushion the shock waves of the confrontation of absolute God-power and absolute Evil.

You will see come out of this year—as you approach it with Serapis Bey's dispensation—great miracles, great acceleration. And after all, it is for the opening of the crown chakra under that hierarchy. And perfect love is the way to raise up perfect wisdom through the resurrection flame, and perfect love is the only way the sons of God have ever defeated the Nephilim and their councils of war.

I AM Maitreya in the heart of the *I* where the cross of the *t* is the formation of a Mother's heart. I AM the ray of the Mother's light manifesting within you.¹³ I AM forever with the Mother on the cross of life. I hold her in the embrace of love, as I hold you, my very own most beloved.

In the name of the entire Spirit of the Great White Brotherhood, I seal this retreat into the heart of the resurrection flame. I seal *you* in the heart of God! I seal the mystical body of God in the heart of Alpha! Lo, he is come. Lo, he is come. And it is done. It is sealed. It is finished.

April 19, 1981
Camelot
Los Angeles County, California

Maitreya knows the question of thy heart.
Maitreya knows the doubt.
Maitreya knows the worlds that thou shalt conquer.
Maitreya knows the perfection of the rose of light
in that very soul appearing.

CHAPTER 12

The Visitation of the Stars

The light of the far-off worlds is come to you! For I AM come in the visitation of the stars, and I would establish coordinates among you of these very far-off worlds, that the light of Sirius and the light of the Pleiades might find amplification in your hearts, O beloved Keepers of the Flame.[1]

Therefore, let it be! Let the channels of light be opened! Let the starry body of thy Self appear! Let us go forth together to transcend worlds, even spirals in distress, even signals that are less than the fullness of the Cosmic Christ that I AM and that you shall be when you see me as I AM.

I AM come for the visitation of the stars. Who are they? Sons of light, fiery flaming ones who always and always atone for the lesser evolution of life.

Piercing yellow fire—I pass my hand over the worlds. And lo, the hand of God releases wisdom, and it doth appear as the going forth of the message of the Great White Brotherhood.

Therefore, we are well pleased that certain souls of light have held the line against their own oncoming karmic retribution, against their own darkness. Holding that line as the focal point of service unto us, our service then becomes the holding of the line for thee, blessed hearts. The secret of attainment is to start, to enter the project with joy, to pursue the impossible, and to watch the explosion of the starry body within!

I Release the Fervor of New Levels of My Own Sphere of Wisdom

I AM Maitreya, marking the sign of the cross. I AM the flame of the Mother in the *I* where I AM and where you are. I AM a golden fire bursting illumination's flame! And I AM determined, in this hour of solstice, to now augment the fire of ascension flame and to bring another momentum of illumination to multiply the action and the penetration of the ruby ray, the love fire of Serapis Bey in this fourteen-month spiral of the stations of the cross.[2]

Let us pass now from the etheric to the mental quadrant, and let us pursue with all gusto the initiatic presence of Helios and Vesta. Let us align with pure love and pure wisdom, and let the marriage of the Lamb be—where I AM, where you are—the magnificence of God appearing.[3]

Lo, I affirm it! And I release a new dynamism of my causal body, subject unto the will of Lord Gautama. Yes, I release the fervor of new levels of my own sphere of wisdom as the manifestation of the wise dominion of a chela on the Path in the heart of the earth and throughout the immortal spheres of the galaxies.

I AM that chela! I will always be the chela of the almighty Word. Lo, I AM THAT I AM! And I AM in the flaming center of the Word suspended there in that center, that vacuum, that spaceless/timeless point of infinity.

Thus is the suspension of thy life in the sphere—in the mighty sphere of God's own being. And in that sphere, which itself is infinity, thou dost approach the point of living contact with the living flame, the point of the opening unto Brahman and the Word. Activating principle, activating force of all being is that Word.

I AM the Buddha Becoming the Buddha Where Thou Art

Maitreya knows the question of thy heart. Maitreya knows the doubt. Maitreya knows the worlds that thou shalt conquer. Maitreya knows the perfection of the rose of light in that very soul appearing.

O magnificence of love, what new world wilt thou conquer? Wilt thou go forth to bind the Adversary and thrust him from the way of the Inner Retreat? Wilt thou enter the heart of the Mother in the mountain, in the sanctuary of our love? Wilt thou see the New Day and the dawn of the new civilization? I say, Yes!

I affirm ongoing spirals of victory! I widen the vistas of a new horizon, of a planetary home that is soon to be elevated, accelerated, raised in the sacred fires of resurrection's flame. How will this be accomplished? It will be by the green shoot—evidence that there is new life!

Thus, come forth. Thus, *be.* There is a process of life becoming life—photosynthesis. Thus, life within you, absorbing cosmic rays and all of the vastness of God, becomes a single cell of identity.

I AM affirming that I AM Maitreya in the very physical body of the messenger and ye all. I AM affirming the lowering of my being into physical dimensions not heretofore penetrated by myself. For I desire to disturb the dust! I desire to quiver the very streambeds of a planetary home and the beds where the dead sleep and must be awakened to life—eternal life or eternal damnation, as the prophet has written.[4] It is so!

Therefore, I AM here and I AM there. And I AM nowhere more apparent than in the sealed interval of the heart, the sealed chamber where there is that point, that replica of the Great Central Sun.

I will be where I will be! For I AM the Buddha becoming the Buddha where thou art. I AM the fire of illumination, and I will not be turned back! For I AM on assignment from Lord Gautama Buddha, who calls me for an acceleration of the ten-year plan[5] of his own causal body of life and does admonish me to initiate you in the path of your own selflessness whereby you discover the Great God Self.

There Is Resilience Born of the Fiery Trial

So magnificent thou art, O God, within these souls of light! Surrender, sacrifice, and service—so even the test of the ten[6] will be the fulfillment of the chelas of the will of God upon earth whereby the nucleus is formed and a community worldwide is wrought.

We can do it! And we know it! For we have measured the measure of the heart of our chelas. We know that there is a unison. There is a consonance. There is a merging of a body of lightbearers upon earth whose hearts are in harmony with our vibration, emanating from this point of light in the heart of the messengers ascended and unascended.

Therefore, we see that lines of force can be drawn! And when they are tested, they are taut. There is strength. There is resilience born of the fiery trial. And there is not that reserve and rigidity that marks the fallen ones or those on the lesser path of self-fulfillment. There is strength and resilience! For everyone upon the planetary body who is one in the harmony of this consonance of eternal life, *there* is the contact with the Great White Brotherhood! *There* is the strengthening of the bond! *There* is the world body! *There* is that mighty framework of life to which all souls of light may rise!

I AM the light of the eternal Ma! I AM the light of the Guru! I AM the light of far-off worlds within you, and I come for integration by the eighth ray!

Be Humble before the Law of Thine Own Being

Keepers of the Flame, you have come on a journey. You have come to where the heart of Maitreya is. Your coming to Camelot is symbolic of your inner journey to the Royal Teton Retreat, where we have gathered in this past week for the fulfillment of an inner spiral of cosmic purpose that has to do with the sealing of our Inner Retreat and the arcing of the light of the Royal Teton Retreat—there to meet now the rainbow rays from the heart of Shamballa, now the flame of Gautama Buddha.[7]

Thus, arcs of light converge! And in the converging is the marking of the sign of the cross, even the place prepared for your own initiation unto the ascension from that holy mount—the mount of the mighty I AM Presence.

Go to! Go thou also as Christ has gone before thee, and recognize the magnanimous heart of my own son Lanello where thou art. Recognize that heart—the open door to your own heart and heart's love, the beloved Christ Self.

Maitreya would have you for a cosmic feast! Maitreya would assimilate and be assimilated. In yesteryear, ye would not. But this is another turn. Have no fear! For when you come this close to me, the wrath of the Buddha itself must consume that fear.

Therefore, be humble before the law of thine own being. This law is able to make permanent the atom of self or to nullify it in an instant. This law is the fullness of God made manifest.

Come into the Circle of the Wide Arm of the Brotherhood

How often do mankind exclaim upon earth, in beholding the workings of the simple laws of physics or chemistry, the very law of God, the very *antahkarana* of life?[8] How often do they exclaim in the very midst of a simple physical experiment, "Behold, God!

God is the Law! God is in his Law! God is present in the very atoms of being"?

How often? Very seldom, blessed ones. For the conceptualization of Deity itself is so distorted, and man has made gods of human forms instead of perceiving the divine form within, without, beyond the veil of the human consciousness. Indeed, all is divine when the consciousness of the beholder is divine. But the consciousness can make of the sublime even the ridiculous and the sordid and the pornographic.

Blessed hearts, notice how the fallen ones have no other design or image to desecrate save even that of the living Christ. They take the most noble beauty and tear the veil of holy innocence from it and therefore make that which is divinity even an object of lust. Thus, life is topsy-turvy on earth. Life is upside down! And we would right it again!

Therefore, come. Come into the circle of the wide arm of the Brotherhood. Come into the mountain retreat.

A Meditation upon the Heart—The Golden Spiral of Life
"Let It Be!"

Let us begin with a meditation upon the heart. Let us pursue the golden spiral of life.

I would sit with you and ponder for a moment even the very intricacy of God. Will you not close your eyes, that you might penetrate deeply into the inner space of thine own heart.

In this stillness I re-create for you, beloved, the noble mansion of thy soul. Here is thy heaven. Here is thy earth. Thou art, as it were, God. For God is the center of this spherical interval, and you are in the center—one.

Here we affirm the mantra:

I and my Father are one. I and my Mother are one.

Thus, I draw the circle around the center. And you are not alone, yet the only awareness that you have of life itself is indeed your own God Self-awareness.

At first there is an uncomfortability in such aloneness. But by daily practice and the exercise of the heart you will begin to value this space of the Buddha, untampered with by man's concepts of time yet by frequencies of eternity, compartmentalized for the absorption of a vast light that is sealed in the single point in the center of the sphere.

Now be seated in that center and position thyself. See the white-fire dot coming into alignment with your own heart chakra.

Now sing with me this mantra. Let it be played upon our instruments, that we might flow with the tone of Alpha: I and my Father are one. I and my Mother are one.

I and my Father are one. I and my Mother are one.
I and my Father are one. I and my Mother are one.
[Sung eight times]

There is far more to this mantra than you can even imagine in your outer mind. For the fullness of manifestation in all degrees of consciousness within thy being comes about through the entering into the center of the spiral and there converging, inverting the light, but never perverting any formula of the sacred fire. Thus, penetrating downward and around and upward again, this mighty flow of inner God-realization ultimates in the manifestation where I AM of Alpha and Omega, worlds without end.

Let us continue the mantra, pouring love—the most intense white fire—into the sphere of Alpha and Omega, now congruent in the etheric octave with your own heart, beloved ones.

For this is why I AM here—to extend starry bodies of far-off worlds within the vastness of my own being, each star the coordinating point of Alpha and Omega. Where there is the fervent heart, the fervor of your heart will magnify the intense white-fire glow. Let it be!

I and my Father are one. I and my Mother are one.
I and my Father are one. I and my Mother are one.
[Sung six times]

I approach nearer, then. And I come for the sealing of the point of light in the center of the sphere of thy being. I seal, by the meshing of worlds, your inner heart, your heart flame, and this fiery-sun point of light.

I seal the figure-eight flow. And each time you enter into this meditation you may visualize the twin spheres of the figure eight and of the eighth ray merging as one—as the white-fire/blue-fire sun.

Now you are the chela of white fire! Now you are the chela of dazzling, blue perfection! Let the merging of the diamond and the sapphire of the heart of Morya be for the merging of the white-fire/blue-fire sun of the God Star, Sirius.

O invisible light rays! O sweetness of celestial spheres! I dedicate these hearts and the invisible sun in the center thereof to the consonance of the eternal Word, to the continuity of Brahman through the Word, through all of life. I dedicate twin spheres to the victory of your path.

Let it be! It is all that I ask.

July 1, 1981
Camelot
Los Angeles County, California

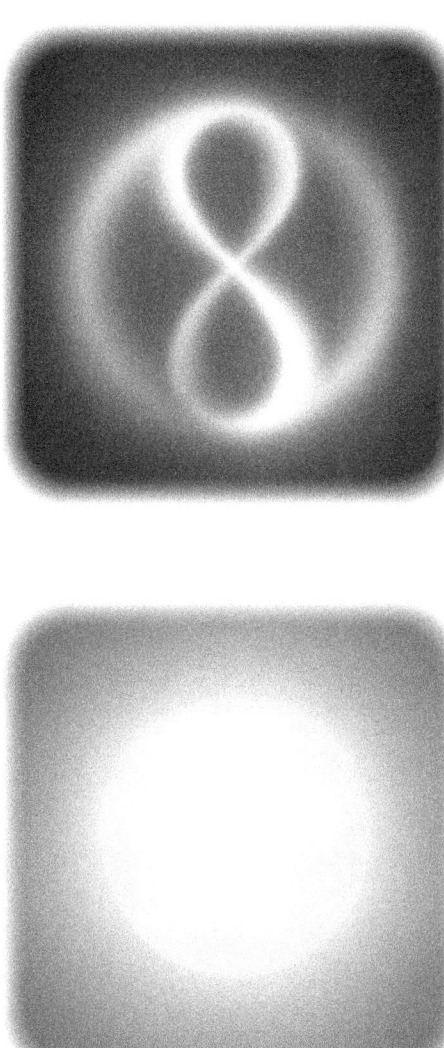

*I AM one with you as you arrive
at the vibration of that light,
as your soul is lifted up,
as there is purification.
And the crystal stream becomes
thy very own Self-awareness.*

CHAPTER 13

The Dispensation of the Righteous Branch

Hail, O eternal, never-ending Word! Hail, O light hidden in the heart, now unveiled! May the lumination of the eternal Christ planted as a seed in the heart by the Divine Mother now grow and expand, that the seed itself planted there might bear witness of the righteous Branch.[1]

From the Tree of Life out of the heart of the I AM Presence descends the Son who is Branch, who is Light, who is your very own perpetual Word. It is the unendingness, as the very nature of that Word of which I would speak. For the ever-flowing stream, the crystal clear water, is a stream of consciousness ordained in the Beginning that is thy life, thy Self, the manifestation of God who is in thee and thy very self. Within this stream of eternal life, I AM.

I AM Maitreya, the Cosmic Christ, entertaining, enfolding, including in my own God-awareness the perpetual flow of the stream of God's consciousness. Therefore I AM one with you as you arrive at the vibration of that light, as your soul is lifted up, as there is purification. And the crystal stream becomes thy very own Self-awareness.

Arriving, then, at the pure River of Life, you understand the meaning of the fount as cause and that which goeth forth from the fount as effect. And therefore in one you experience the Father and the Son and you know that these twain cannot be separated but must forever be one.

The Place Prepared

I have heard and I AM the Word that is spoken in your midst.[2] Truly it is the vibration of Sanat Kumara, by the heart of Archangel Gabriel unto Jeremiah, that I would preserve within you. For Jeremiah's time is also come, and his reappearing in this age will also mark the fulfillment of his own self-prophecy.[3] And you will see that this son of light will be born again, and you will realize that as your heart is one with the stream of his consciousness, you will be found in the ratio of the golden-ratio spiral unto his mighty God flame.

You will understand the meaning of the Inner Retreat as the Place Prepared for this son of light and avatars of light who cannot be born on unhallowed ground, even as those in Judah had to exit the city, for it was made unhallow and therefore was not able to be dwelt in. So it is with the cities of earth—the avatars who are to come may not touch the unsanctified ground.

"Holiness to the LORD"[4] is the sign of our people. That holiness is always the place prepared in the heart, where the very intense ray of the I AM Presence can manifest in the earth and perform that mighty work that is the answer to the call.

Call upon the LORD! Call upon the name, the sacred name I AM THAT I AM, Sanat Kumara! Call upon it unto the cycles of the day and the night for the appearing of the Holy City[5] and the fiery nucleus of the Inner Retreat.

Call for the mighty sword of life to now raise up all who are of the righteous Branch[6] and of the priests of Levi.[7] For their number must be multiplied in this community, even as the serpents are cast out. For they cast themselves out by nonalignment with the living Word.

The Mighty Work of the Ages

In the invincible light of God-freedom, I stand. For it is by the very nature of the eternality of the Word and the invincibility of the light, the constancy of the promise, the certainty of this prophecy, this note fulfilled, that we will stand and we will conquer.

All of earth puts forth the vibration of decay, disintegration, uncertainty, and doubt. Doubt, then, is the breaking and the crumbling of the former matrix. But we come to build! We come to plant upon the sacred stone, where God is.[8] Be that stone! Understand the foundation! Understand how all things now become physical because you have the ray of illumination. It is indeed the ray of hope! It is indeed the ray of vision!

By enlightenment you see clearly. By the vision of the mountain you head for it, you make your way there, you converge at the Royal Teton Retreat! There you come! There you understand the meaning of this heart chamber of God, this place of the descent of the root races, this home of archangels and of Gautama Buddha. You understand the necessity for establishing the outer focus of Shamballa[9] and you see clearly the need for the inner and the outer manifestation to be close at hand. I look for the fulfilling of the vision, that we might then perform together the mighty work of the ages. Let us begin anew.

The Revolution of Sanat Kumara

I place my hand upon the forehead of those who would be initiated further in the service of the World Teachers. I seal all who will hear again and again the word of Jeremiah and take unto themselves this fire infolding itself, even this descent of the I AM THAT I AM. It is not only a gift of prophecy but it is a gift of the future that is become the present. It is the gift of the descent of your own causal body and all that was ordained from the beginning for you to fulfill in your individual divine plan.

Thus have we tarried. Thus does the light go forth from the altar.

And all who are so blessed will understand the need, now, for us to send forth souls of light for the revolution of Sanat Kumara. It is called the Woman's Revolution.[10] But the sign of the Woman clothed with the Sun is the sign of the coming of the Guru, the sign of the eternal Mother flame in the person of the Ancient of Days returned to the very center of the chelas of that fire.

Therefore, beloved, it is a revolution of the sons and daughters of Sanat Kumara. And it is called the Woman's Revolution, for truly it is the initiation of the light of Maitreya, my own flame. And it is a dear flame given to me by God.

This initiation of my flame and of the Mother light is for the perpetual flowing from you of the mystical seed of the Cosmic Christ as the preaching and the teaching, as the covenant come again, even written in the inward parts of the soul and the chakras and in the heart and in the living temple of our God. All these things are fulfilled where the mind and heart of the chela meet Sanat Kumara.

The meeting place of heaven and earth is in the Word that flows, in the Word incarnate. Where the Word is precipitated in Matter, where you stand at that point of the delivery of the Word, there is this meeting place, there is its sending. And we send you by the light of the Faithful and True.[11] For as we have said, there is a war ongoing out there, outside of this circle of fire. We send you, then, to defeat the fallen priests, not only of Judah and Israel but of Lemuria and Atlantis—the very same ones who have fallen by their misuse of the light of the Mother, the eternal flame of Sanat Kumara.

It Is the Age of the Divine Right of the Woman and Her Seed

Come forth, Mighty Victory! Anoint those souls of light who will go forth in America to counteract the feminist revolt against the living God and the fallen ones who would raise up the perversion of the life force and declare it to be the norm of life, and therefore by that very act to set the seal upon America of the internal destruction of Sodom and Gomorrah.

Let these fallen ones be exposed! Let the truth be heard! And let the lambs of God now put on the mantle of the Lamb. Let the sacred sword of Jeremiah *be* in your hand! And let us defeat these individuals who spread lies abroad, who infiltrate families and the home, mothers and fathers, children and education, bringing forth their godless philosophy of the Nephilim in this age called "humanism" (to give it that sense of innocuousness. For who in defending humanism could possibly be against human beings? And, after all, is not this age one of human rights?)

Well, we have gone over this ground before. It is the age of the divine right of the woman and her seed.[12] It is the age of the divine right of the righteous Branch and of the light itself. It is the age of righteousness.

I Champion the Light of the Raising of the Mother Flame within You

Let the unrighteous leader be cast down! I denounce him as sitting in the seat of the throne of David, where he has not the authority of the Word![13] Let the exposure come about! Let it be known! For I AM in the very heart of the Lord God Sanat Kumara and I come for the purging, that the true Son of God might be raised up.

Let the seed, then, of the Son of light become the foundation of a new city, a new understanding, and truly a new mission. Let those who in their hearts bear the banner of the World Teachers, my sons Jesus and Kuthumi, stump* for the revolution of the Coming Buddha who is come. Let them stump for the light and against the anti-light. Let the lines be drawn.

---
*to participate in a traveling lecture tour

Let there be a very specific manifesto of this Woman's Revolution,[14] stating the case of the divine right of the true woman of God and those rights that can never be given to the fallen ones, which they seek to take unto themselves, having not earned them on the path of light.

There is a sharpening of the tongue of the LORD. It is a two-edged sword. You will bear it! You will be it! You will transmit my fire! For I, Maitreya, with the banner of the World Mother, do champion and enter the fray.

I champion the light of the raising of the Mother flame within you, the prophecy of the fulfillment of Israel. I champion your word as my word, as the message of Sanat Kumara. We come for the manifesto of Alpha and Omega. We come that all may read clearly, simply, that which is of the light and that which is not. Let the preaching and the publishing of the Word be for the rallying of the hosts of the LORD and the judgment of the fallen ones!

Let the dance of the virgin souls of my people truly be the dance of Shiva. And let the Holy Spirit be felt now! Now, therefore, I send it as the portion of my own being upon you. Upon all who can receive it, the portion of my own Spirit *is* upon you! I breathe it forth and I transfer the sacred breath.

Purusha.

The Hand of Saint Germain Is upon the Governments and the Economies of the Nations

My dispensation and my anointing shall be, for all time and space, for those who come under the dispensation of the righteous Branch. I AM the Cosmic Christ representative, very much a part of this community, very much a part of the day-to-day plans for the Inner Retreat.

Make haste to divest yourselves of those things of this world that are excess baggage. Let the alchemy of the sacred fire transmute them into supply that may be laid upon the foundation of the city we would build. Yes, it is an inner city. Yes, it is an outer city, being a citadel and a fortress unto the lovers of God.

I am with you now for the victory. And I watch the signs of the watchman of the night, Saint Germain, who places his hand as the right hand of the age upon the governments and the economies of the nations. His right hand as the prophet of Israel is upon this and every nation and upon the fallen ones in their meetings and upon those who would betray the people. The hand of Saint Germain is upon them! And he does hold them and stay the action of their wickedness, that the faithful and true followers of the light might now enter into the very streets of the earth and command life free by truth and its sword!*

I AM in the Amen and in the heart of the Aum. I AM Maitreya, Mother flame in action!

[20-second pause]

It is an exercise of stillness to be in the heart of the Christ and the Buddha. It is an exercise of action to go forth and implement the Word.

Bless you for your constancy in the yin and the yang of life whereby we are able to bring to you, Keepers of the Flame, the deeper mysteries of life.

You are our First Love.

July 19, 1981
Camelot
Los Angeles County, California

---

*i.e., the sacred Word

*I AM evolving in every heart,
through every Christ Self,
through every threefold flame.
And when I say "I AM," it is the office I hold.
It is the Cosmic Christ of which I AM aware.*

CHAPTER 14

The Living Book

I would speak to you of the Passion Week[1] from the level of the Cosmic Christ and the very personal relationship of the ascended Guru with the unascended chela, who must shortly pass through this initiation.

Truly the flow of hearts—the oneness of our hearts—on that occasion is something that the world must know and be aware of. As Jesus called me Father, as I served in the office of Father closest to him, so through my heart, which kept the vigil of his entire mission, he was one with Gautama, with Sanat Kumara, with Alpha, and therefore he understood the One Sent.[2] He understood the messenger in heaven as the messenger on earth and as the very extension of the divine light, who is God.

Thus, as to me, Jesus was an extension in form of my life. And as each one above me in the offices of hierarchy was thus considered the same, we all partook of his cup as the Great Law would allow. For one part of life—especially when that part of the light is the living, pulsating, manifestation of the Cosmic Christ—can only be experienced by every other part of life who is Cosmic Christ as the essence of one's Self.

This unity, beloved, this feeling of every part of life that is part of God everywhere, is something that is dulled to your own outer awareness, not because you are sinners but because you are here in form with many tasks to perform in order to prepare this manger for the birth of every avatar to come.

Thus, if you were to retain the world pain, the ongoing world crucifixion of the Christed ones, you would then, perforce, be required to sit in meditation, like the statue of the Buddha or of Padma Sambhava. For only in perpetual meditation and in the giving forth of the science of the spoken Word does one hold the balance for this experience of the oneness of the mystical body of God.

Therefore, activities change on the ascending scale of hierarchy. But remember also that Lord Confucius, one of great attainment and light, keeps himself entirely active in the service at the Royal Teton Retreat while yet maintaining a certain awareness of life becoming life through the cosmic travail of the woman.[3]

I myself, in this understanding that I have shared with you, was of course one in the very heart and the pierced side, the full experience of the Lord Christ. And I can tell you that the ongoing invective of the fallen ones, endured by the lightbearers over the centuries, is just as great as the final conclusion in the physical octave, and perhaps greater. For as you know and as Jesus has told you, the brief period upon the cross for him was not nearly the suffering that some saints have experienced lifetime after lifetime.

This he said. And therefore let none accuse him of disparaging his own office or his own dispensation of the crucifixion. This he has not done, nor have you. But only for the glorification of the Son, wherever that Son does appear, is the Lord Jesus Christ come, and every other avatar whom I have sponsored.

The Initiation of the Crucifixion

In contemplation of this Passion Week, then, we approach it not from the sorrowful way of the fourteen stations of the cross, but moreover as profound instruction, as illumination of the Lord Christ by the Holy Spirit so that each one may squarely understand what he may expect as he sets his heart to the true path of original Christhood.

"Be of good cheer, for I have overcome the world!"[4] He spake those words of mine as I spoke them to him, giving unto him the good cheer of my office and attainment, reassuring him for the victory. In so many of the phrases that you now read by this illumination in scripture, you will feel the vibration of the golden thread of illumination, of the quietness of the Buddha. The yellow fire is a quiet yet all-powerful strength emanating continually the Word as affirmation of being.

The initiation of the crucifixion—which means the fastening of oneself to the cross of Alpha and Omega, to be where there is the convergence of the Father-Mother light—this, beloved hearts, is a calling and a selection that you would not want to miss in this embodiment.

I urge you, then, to consider the strengthening of your individual forces in God preparing you day by day. As you receive again and again communion,* so the crumb of life is a "crumb," a portion of the whole loaf of initiation until you can truly take in the fullness of the body and blood of the ascended master presence, your own archetype in heaven—Jesus, Saint Germain, El Morya—and can contain that light and that being where you are.

And What Is the Path?
The Path Is the Passion Week

I AM Maitreya. For I AM in the heart of the mountain, at the very edge of the wilderness here in this place consecrated to Ephraim's sons.[5]

---

*This may mean the ritual of receiving Holy Communion, as in the Catholic Church, and/or one's communion with the inner Christ.

I AM here for the reinforcing of the circle of Lord Gautama.[6] I AM here to remind and anoint you of the desire of Serapis Bey and the hosts of the fourth ray to implant a mighty focus of the white fire of the Mother.

But caution given from on high must be reiterated. These servants of the fourth ray of purity have said: We will not accelerate this focus here lest this very light encourage greater opposition to itself, and lest those who support it faint in the very process of defending it.

The word has also been given that certain avatars will not embody here until those who comprise the community have sufficient attainment to hold the balance for that light—not because these avatars are afraid but because they would not jeopardize your own path. And what is the Path? The Path is this—the Passion Week, the understanding of all that it holds for you personally.

The Place Prepared

Thus, the building of the Inner Retreat[7] is so important in the physical octave because of the loss of the children of light on this planet and because of the physical door being the only door by which they can enter before they move on to etheric octaves.

This, being so important, then, must not become so overly important that you yourself allow the work of the day or of the hour to interfere with the sense of the inner building of the temple, your own temple, so reinforced by the white stone of light—brick upon brick, these stones that must one day hold the full effulgent light of the Lord Sanat Kumara. It is a respite for the Mother and for all who come here to dwell in this Place Prepared. Realize, then, that it is also a sacrifice to go out from this place and to descend once again into the area where world thought and a concentrated world population reinforce the negative aspects of Antichrist.

Remember that only a few individuals having conscious hatred may funnel the hatred of ten million people living in the Los Angeles area. Even if only fifty harbored resentment or malice toward the messengers or the students or the Church, they are sufficient as transformers of the full momentum of world hatred.

Therefore, you see, it has always been the path of the avatars to remove themselves from areas of density of population, and then beyond that to hide themselves in places where no one could find them or know their exact location. For when [the location of the avatar is known, the individuals who funnel hatred] will always place the crosshairs of a focus of the cross itself exactly where the physical anchor point of the avatar is, in order to further direct that same energy of world hatred.

The Sign of Mobility

Thus it is necessary for the sign of mobility to be realized in the advanced chela as the sign of safety. And it is often necessary to remove oneself to a point in the Inner Retreat, here or there, where only the birds and the angels and the elementals may truly know the forcefield of your own presence.

Realize that there are little ones who live in tiny bodies, and there are little children connected with this activity who rightfully ought not to be in an area of such dense populations. Often they are weary and burdened and sometimes even out of sorts for bearing so much momentum of world energy.

Let all who are a part of this community—parents and teachers and those who have concern about their own path of light—realize that as the way of the messengers of God has been shown, and this one also, so you must follow. For your day is also coming, and the days will be shortened for you who elect to adopt the full path of Christhood, when you yourselves will no longer be able to bear the burden of the areas of large concentrations of the population.

It is then that you will require the Place Prepared and you will understand why the sacrifice is necessary. Each sacrifice you make, then, is your own surety against the day of the Lord's calling to bear more light and therefore more world karma, and to be in a place where added unto this there may simply not be the intensity of lifewaves uncommitted to the solar evolution of the Cosmic Christ.

And what is this solar evolution, my beloved? I AM evolving in every heart, through every Christ Self, through every threefold flame. And when I say "I AM," it is the office I hold. It is the Cosmic Christ of which I AM aware. For no one can contain the fullness of that Christ, yet I hold the office and the mantle. The Cosmic Christ is the universal presence of the Word springing forth, budding, and taking root here and there. Thus, you see, because I hold the office, I AM there when each avatar is born, when you are born the new creature,[8] when you also elect to be upon the cross.

The Word in Yourselves Becomes the Judgment

I urge you, as I have already done through this messenger of my heart, that you contemplate in these seven days [of the Passion Week]—and the eighth day, which signifies the eternal rest from time and space—these events in the life of one who has so portrayed to you that which is necessary. Not having drunk the full cup, I can only tell you that to ascend prematurely would be a mighty disappointment. For each and every one of you, as stalwart sons and disciples of the World Mother, longs for the fullness of that sacred fire and that calling.

Because they have done unto him what they would, you place yourself also in the place of John the Baptist and Jesus, saying, "So also now is come the judgment of this world. For judgment

I AM come, and yet I judge not. There is one that judgeth, and it is the Word that I speak."[9]

Dear hearts, you have seen this Word in yourselves become the judgment of those to whom you have spoken it. When the Word has spoken through you and the Holy Spirit has passed from you, you know surely that this is the extension of the Guru Sanat Kumara in your presence. And you know that surely in the end, whatever "the end" means in terms of that individual, the judgment is come; the judgment has exacted the full penalty of the Law for the rejection of the Godhead dwelling bodily in you.

You Are Always at the Alchemy of Change

Now, blessed hearts, you cannot flaunt the Law and be off guard and have even a twinge of pride that you are somehow better than others, and then go and speak your own mind and piece and say, "It is the judgment." Great, great humility is required of those who are the instrument of the Word. You may be the instrument of a message of God one day to one soul, but if you are out of alignment for the next thirty days or thirty years, the Word will not speak again.

And so there is a daily striving, a tuning of the instrument. You must become a virtuoso on the instrument of God that is your body temple. Would you suspect that a first violinist would perform with a symphony orchestra or play passages alone before large audiences without daily practice, over and over again, and the tuning of the strings?

Thus, because you have won a battle, do not become overly certain, overly confident, and think that somehow you have arrived and nothing can change. You are always at the alchemy of change. You are always at the altar. You are always in the process of transcending that former state. It is like being in the perpetual war of Armageddon, the battle victorious.

If you are on a certain ground and there your position becomes known and you fight the enemy there, and then on another day and another round the enemy is upon you, would you remain in the same place of the previous battle now that the enemy has defined your point of strategy and of reference? Why, not so. You would take yourself and your band to another place.

So, you see, as soon as the enemy defines your state of consciousness, as soon as the enemy has, so to speak, "your number"—which is your vibration and the formula of your being—as soon as you have the victory there, you must no longer be found there. You must be one niche higher on the scale of initiation so that when they seek and look for you in the old familiar place, you are not there.

They could not find Jesus until he desired to be found and desired to be taken. He made it relatively simple for Judas to betray him, for the hour had come for the Son of man to be glorified.[10]

Thus, beloved hearts, you may be certain that we have a mighty work in store for you, and thus be not tempted that somehow the hour is come for you for a physical change or a physical trial or a physical death—even those who occupy temples of an older age.

This is the point of Serapis Bey, where you are so enfired with the white light and the victory of eternal life that you never submit in consciousness to any projection of the removal of yourself, by divine dispensation or otherwise, to other spheres or octaves. For heaven descends to the lowest level of the physical and astral planes through you, for heaven desires the total victory in this age.

America Is Undergoing the Passion Week

The forces of the world are gathering. The Christ crucified is America. And America as a people and a nation know not that they are undergoing the Passion Week—and the enemy is within—within the very temple, and without.

Both the Pharisees and the Caesars of Rome have decreed the destruction of this initiate, [this messenger.] Suffice it to say that the remnant of Christed ones, the anointed in her midst who come from all nations, must take upon themselves this national crucifixion and spread the word of the betrayal of the fallen ones and even the betrayal of those who are among the disciples of Christ in the churches.

Only if the people are informed as to the Son of man within them and of their own Path—how to find it, how to walk it, how to achieve it—can the nation as a whole rise victorious on resurrection morn. It is indeed, then, the hour of the ascended masters breaking the bread of life through you, through all who go forth publishing the Word, preaching the Word.

All who are a part of this entire pyramid of the establishment of our activity, each one serving, makes possible the delivery of our publications, a single book into the heart of one who has so cried out and who has so longed for truth that that very longing has established the equivalent vibration in polarity of the seraphim, to whom you call to bring those souls to the stores to find those books.

Blessed ones, think of the fervor of the soul as a seeker for the Path who contains enough light to attract the seraphim so that that soul might be escorted to find a book that to you has been a long-ago stepping stone on the Path, a book perhaps you no longer think about for you have eaten it, chewed it up, assimilated it, and you have become the living book.

The Teachings of Enoch

The treasure of the book and the many books written by your father Enoch is still held within the very heart of the earth. Three hundred sixty-six books did Enoch write in the presence of God when he was taken up to the highest heaven.[11] But after this, the Flood came, and no one yet has found these lost books of Enoch. Yet they were read by his children before the coming of the Flood.

I desire you to understand that all of heaven has conspired together to deliver the Word of God, which God gave to Enoch through these two witnesses.[12] For this teaching given to Enoch was for you personally, for all the descendants of light who came through Adam and reincarnated again, for every embodied angel who embodied for the rescue of the lightbearers. And these teachings, now published in these publications, are the very message that God secured through Enoch before his ascension into heaven.

I pray that you will pursue a study of this text of the Secrets of Enoch and that you will realize how close you are to that ascended master,[13] how dearly he, as father and father figure in your midst, loves you, and how determined he is to promote your calling, your mission, and the spreading of the word of these books and teachings until all for whom they have been secured may have them and make the choice to ascend to God, as he did.

There is great fervor among all the hosts of the LORD, but there is no greater fervor in any than the fervor of your father Enoch to deliver to you the writings that he himself wrote in the presence of God as his messenger.

You Were All Born to Be Messengers of Shamballa

Do you see how you were all born to be messengers of Shamballa, to carry some portion of that Word—to live it, to internalize it, to be it as a pulsating light on earth? Remember the calling.

Messengers of Maitreya, messengers of Shamballa, I pray that you learn the message well. Shortcut it not, pervert it not, misinterpret it not, but deliver it as the crystal clear stream of your own I AM Presence flowing through you for the nourishing of life.

The message is the cup of cold water, which you give in the name of the Cosmic Christ.

In the name of the beloved Son, Jesus, and all sons of liberty whom the Karmic Board has sent in this century, I seal you by the intense fire of the illumination of my heart and of the Holy Spirit.

And I will touch you now, and by this touch anchor that point whereby you might also receive all that is to be given this Easter week at Camelot.[14]

April 4, 1982
Inner Retreat
Park County, Montana

*I AM Maitreya.
I have sent my messenger before my face.
I do not come with fanfare.
For after all, we have always been
and you have always known me,
and I have not left you.*

CHAPTER 15

In the Heart of the One Sent

Beloved ones, many sorts of individuals on earth have anticipated my coming. They have plotted their charts by their concept of astrology. With psychic predictions and false dictations, they have announced my presence. Some say I embodied. Some say I am embodied in London.[1] Some say I am dictating through this or that one.

I wish to tell you that I AM here in the fullness of my integrity, my Presence, my ascended master light body. And if I am to be embodied, that embodiment is the transfer of my light to the heart of the One Sent. Your Christ Self is the One Sent, and I am one with that Christ. To get to know that Christ is the daily pursuit of the magnitude of God's love, who gave to you that blessed person of your own Real Self.

I AM the practical Buddha who has come with compassion and light and decisiveness to lead my own to a higher octave of service. I am here with the rescue flame of illumination and the mighty sword.

Pictured in the hand of the Mother and not far from right,[2] this bearing of the sword must be against the infamy of the fallen ones who thwart the plan of Confucius and Lord Lanto,[3] who this very new year have presented to Saint Germain and Lord Gautama and the Lords of Karma their offering in the name of the Knight Commander and the God of Freedom* on behalf of America. You will see these two masters come to the fore of your consciousness and lead you on an illumined path so bright that you will soon look upon your former state of consciousness of six months ago as being almost benighted—that is, in the sense of chaos and old night.

For I trust that you still look forward to the knighting by the Lord Christ and of Saint Germain. Some of you do not know that in previous Keeper of the Flame services, some among you received the calling of knighthood through the messenger Mark, and others through the Mother. These initiations have been left off in the very midst of the battle. Some have earned their calling and have not received any approbation in the student body. But the acknowledgment is of our heart. And when a certain of the cloud of battle has passed, you will know who these shining ones are and we may once again transfer the new name of knighthood, which is not the inner name promised in Revelation but a name that refers to a certain virtue extolled.

The Coming into Your Life of My Essence

I AM Maitreya. I have sent my messenger before my face.[4] I do not come with fanfare. For after all, we have always been and you have always known me, and I have not left you.

The great cosmic event anticipated is a foreshadowing and an overshadowing of an individual lifestream with my Presence. But I tell you, these ones [with their psychic predictions and false dictations] have not known of the real meaning of the prophecy, of the messenger, who not only embodies my flame but speaks the word of your own Christhood.

The most important coming into your life of my essence is

---
*The Knight Commander and the God of Freedom is referring to Saint Germain.

the descent of your own Christ Self. Some of you must have a new outlook and a turnaround to truly know the meaning of the Christ mind. Others are so imbued with that Christed consciousness that you scarcely realize the immensity of the light that you carry.

Therefore it is well to imitate those who have gone before and to live in my heart and in the heart of the messengers, until by that very process of the pressing of hearts, you realize—line by line and decision by decision—your own Christhood. Interaction with all life is necessary to the process. For when in the presence of a wrong vibration and infamy and a desecration of the stature of the living God, even the little children learn to know the difference.

This is a planet where very small ones become aware of abortion and murder and all types of unspeakable crimes, diseases, and manifestations of insanity. And, blessed hearts, these pure souls learn more than through their schoolwork in life. They learn, above all, by vibration. They learn by the tone of the voice what is and what is not. They learn by the aura and by contact with your chakras.

Therefore, there is an inner absorbing of patterns, and the only setback occurs when immature souls of a young age are not able to throw off a certain programming and indoctrination that they receive by contact with those who have yet momentums of aggressiveness that cannot be hidden from the little child.

Meditate upon the Buddha to Be Realized by You

I say to you, then, that when you hear of the preaching and the prophecy or the psychic prediction of the coming of Maitreya, "Lo here, or Lo there,"[5] I bid you go to your heart and to your Christ Self, and there meditate upon the Buddha to be realized by you.

The Buddha may exist, but it is that portion of the Buddha that you realize in waking consciousness in this octave that is defined as the Buddha you have *become* in this octave.

Thus, you see, if I were somewhere on a crowded street, on a highway, or in a large city or out in a field, and if I were in the form of a child or a student or an old man or a mother with child, you would not know me unless you had first known me through your own Christ Self.

The importance of the appearing of the Christ in this season, then, is your own perception and externalization of that one. The more you have perceived within, or in our presence in the dictations, the more you have glimpsed of the reality of the identity of the Son of God and the clearer will be the vision to you of the One Sent.

I have already disguised my representatives here and there. Some of you know them and respect them, and some of you know them and ignore them and belittle them. This is to say that your concept of Christ is way off.

Thus, my beloved, the messenger has remained silent, and we are silent also. For what good would it do if I should announce to you that one among you were my representative, one you had criticized or condemned for this or for that?

Now, either you would have to accept my word and deny your criticism and put it into the flame, or you would have to question the messenger as the mouthpiece of my word and think in your heart that perhaps you must go elsewhere to find a true messenger and a true avatar. So you see how idolatrous is the unredeemed consciousness.

Look for the Christ in All People

We do not wish to make it difficult for your path, any more so than you have already made it difficult for yourself. I give you, then, a simple lesson this night. First of all, you have all seen the Christ and have not known him. Second of all, you ought to all look for the Christ in all people. But when you recognize that light of the Christ in a special virtue and service, do not worship it, do not give preferential treatment to that one, do not enter into idolatry, but say to yourself as you pray by your bed at night:

> *My God, I have seen the Christ this day. I have seen the beauty of an act of God in a fellow servant. Now I look to thee, O* L*ORD*, *and I praise thee. I praise the Christ of my own being and I will externalize the same virtue I have glimpsed.*
>
> *I will not try to catch the bird of happiness and clutch him as my own. I will not try to possess another's Christhood and demand it be the saviour of my life. But I will work the works of him that sent me,*[6] *that others who are searching might find in me a refreshing and cool oasis in the desert of life.*
>
> *I will not show too much of my light, neither to offend nor belittle nor engender idolatry in another. But I will give enough—enough so that one may have hope and be nourished in his own quest and one day come to the mighty Tree of Life and realize that the fruit of that tree of his own God consciousness is the only Christhood he will truly know.*

It Is Impossible to Know God Except by His Spirit

I must tell you that most of you do not know one another as you think you do. Some individuals who are close in the human sense almost take pride that they understand another's mind or heart or actions and can anticipate their behavior. These are behaviorists, one and all.

And those who are the godless seek to control others by memorizing their human patterns and then by carefully manipulating the same. But the individual's mannerisms and human behavior do not always tell the secret of the soul or the nature of the inner Christ. Those of the greatest manifestation of my Presence may not be the hail-fellow-well-met—the jolly sort of person whose personality everyone flocks to.

I remember the gurus who were gruff and growling and angry most of the time. And why were they angry? They were angry at the nations and at the planetary momentums of intrigue. And sometimes the sweetest disciples would speak to these gurus and they would answer in a growl and a thrust of anger that would go through the body [of the disciple] like a chill wind. And it was intended so to do, that the bodies of the disciples might become transmitters of this anger to the world, with all of its infamy and evil.

It is impossible to know God except by his Spirit. You may examine character traits. You may think you know exactly what is the definition of Christ and Antichrist. You may be certain you will know both on the highway of life. But unless the Holy Spirit, as the Maha Chohan, reveal it to you, you may be wrong nine times out of ten.

I trust that you have a better score than that, having so often perceived our vibration in these dictations. When all the world is maya and the pinpoints of light are the hearts of the chelas, do you not expect, sometimes, that even the visage of our own best servants should be blurred by the water itself, by the astral plane of illusion, even distorting the most beautiful of countenances? And then, of course, there is the burden of karma, past and planetary, and so many conditions of life. All of this put together does not tell the best of tales concerning the best of men.

Therefore, beloved, let this be the year when illusion drops suddenly to the ground, as a cloak too heavy, and the body is light and clear again and no longer encumbered. Let this be a year, then, when you have no illusions, not of grandeur or of the miserable sinner that is projected upon you. Let us not have illusions about ourselves or others. And most of all, let us not have illusions about the ascended masters, that they might appear as they really are and not as they are imagined to be.

I AM Maitreya, a funny sort of fellow. I, too, look for friends who understand me. I hope that you will. I hope that in your heart of hearts you can perceive me as I am. It is not only your wish to be known and loved for what you are and not for what you are not. It is also the wish of every angel in heaven.

The Things in Life That Are Important

So, beloved, let us get down to the things in life that are important:

- Work on your threefold flame.
- Love your Christ and everyone else's.
- Listen to our words and what they really mean.
- Treasure every communiqué from our octave.
- Love one another as I have loved you and will always love you.
- Remember the prophets, their example, and their precepts.
- Do a good day's work.
- Covet not that which is another's attainment.
- Give freely, but hold fast what thou hast received from God for thine own inner initiation.
- Expose the lie, but dwell upon the image of truth.
- Remember the mild eye of Pallas Athena and behold the nobility of the visage of the Goddess of Liberty, of the Goddess of Truth, of Justice, of Mercy, of Love, of Peace.

How great is the countenance of the women of heaven, who belong solely to God and are independent in their service of the Father and the Son and the Holy Spirit. We are grateful that we can count on the ladies of heaven to assist us in the great work of igniting illumination's flame heart-to-heart around the planet.

The Christ Child is born. Christmas is over. A new year is upon us. Let us see to it that not one incoming avatar of my heart be lost.

January 2, 1983
Camelot
Los Angeles County, California

NOTES*

CHAPTER 1: Initiation for the New Day

1. *The Great Central Sun,* also called "the Great Hub," is the center of cosmos, the point of integration of the Spirit-Matter cosmos. It is the point of integration of physical-spiritual creation, the nucleus, or white-fire core, of the Cosmic Egg.
2. *Saint Germain* is the chohan (Lord) of the seventh ray and the hierarch of the Aquarian age. He is known as the God of Freedom to the earth and sponsored the United States of America. He brought to us the knowledge of the violet flame in order to assist us in the balancing of personal and world karma. He is a most gracious and loving master who initiates souls in the ritual of transmutation through the use of the violet flame by the power of the spoken Word, meditation, and visualization. [See inset "The Sacred Gift of the Violet Flame," pp. 117–21.]
3. *Cosmic Christ* is an office in hierarchy held by the one who keeps the focus of the universal Christ on behalf of all mankind. The Cosmic Christ is the embodiment of the combined momentum of the Christ consciousness of every individual soul evolving in the Matter cosmos. The ascended master Lord Maitreya currently holds this office and demonstrates the cosmic consciousness of the Christ to earth's evolutions and throughout cosmos.
4. *The four lower bodies* are four sheaths consisting of four distinct frequencies that surround the soul—the physical, emotional, mental, and etheric—providing vehicles for the soul in her journey through time and space. The etheric sheath, highest in vibration, is the gateway to the three higher bodies, which are the Christ Self, the I AM Presence, and the causal body.

---

*N.B. Books listed here are published by Summit University Press unless otherwise noted.

5. Luke 9:23.
6. The *I AM THAT I AM* is the individualized Presence of God focused for each individual soul. It is the God-identity of the individual, the Divine Monad, the individual Source. God revealed his name I AM THAT I AM to Moses out of the flaming fire of the bush that burned but was not consumed. [See inset "The Chart of Your Divine Self," pp. 104–09.]
7. *Chela.* In India, a disciple of a religious teacher or guru is called a chela. It is a term generally used to refer to a student of the ascended masters and their teachings. Specifically, it refers to a student of more than ordinary self-discipline and devotion who is initiated by an ascended master and who serves the cause of the Great White Brotherhood.
8. *The path of the ascension* is a spiritual acceleration of consciousness and a process that follows the natural course of spiritual evolution. All of the thoughts, feelings, and deeds from the present and past lives count toward or against the ascension. In taking progressive steps on the spiritual path, one ultimately finds his way back to the heart of God and enters the eternal life.
9. *Hierarchy* is a universal, ordered system in which the members are ranked according to their levels of spiritual attainment and divine awareness. It consists of beings on earth and throughout cosmos who identify with God's consciousness and embody a certain aspect of that awareness. Hierarchy is based on pure standards of spiritual attainment and evolution in consciousness. It is the ideal upon which the earthly standards of hierarchy were originally founded.
10. *The dark night of the soul* and *the dark night of the Spirit.* The dark night of the soul is experienced as one encounters the return of personal karma. This dark night of the soul is in preparation for the dark night of the Spirit, when the soul is cut off from the I AM Presence and must survive solely on the light garnered in the heart while holding the balance for planetary karma.
11. *Cosmic consciousness* is defined as God's awareness of himself in and as the cosmos. It is man's awareness of himself as he lives, moves, and has being within the spheres of God's cosmic Self-awareness.
12. *The Path:* The strait gate and narrow way that leadeth unto Life. (Matt. 7:14) The path of initiation whereby the disciple who

pursues the Christ consciousness overcomes step-by-step the limitations of selfhood in time and space and attains reunion with Reality through the ritual of the ascension.
13. Rev. 3:8.
14. See John 21:15–17.
15. *The Christ consciousness* is the consciousness or awareness of the self in and as the Christ; the attainment of a level of consciousness commensurate with that which was realized by Jesus, the Christ. The Christ consciousness is the realization within the soul of that mind which was in Christ Jesus. (Phil. 2:5)
16. *The sacred labor* is that particular calling, livelihood or profession whereby one establishes his soul's worth both to himself and to his fellowman. One perfects his sacred labor by developing his God-given talents as well as the gifts and graces of the Holy Spirit and laying these upon the altar of service to humanity.
17. *Sanat Kumara* [Sanskrit, "always a youth"] is the Ancient of Days spoken of in Daniel 7:9, 13, 22. He is the Great Guru of the seed of Christ throughout cosmos, and initiates us on the path of the ruby ray.
18. John 8:58.
19. *The Divine Mother* is also known as the Universal Mother and Cosmic Virgin. The Divine Mother is the feminine polarity of the Godhead, the manifestation of God as Mother.
20. *Kundalini* [Sanskrit, "coiled-up serpent"]: The sacred fire that lies like a coiled serpent in the base-of-the-spine chakra. It is also referred to as the light of the Divine Mother. When the Kundalini is awakened, it rises through the spinal column to the crown chakra, quickening each of the other chakras on the way.
21. *World Teacher.* The office in hierarchy held by those ascended beings whose attainment qualifies them to represent the universal and personal Christ to unascended mankind. The office of World Teacher, formerly held by Maitreya, was passed to Jesus and his disciple Saint Francis (now the ascended master Kuthumi) on January 1, 1956. Serving under Lord Maitreya, Jesus and Kuthumi are responsible for setting forth the teachings in this two-thousand-year cycle leading to individual self-mastery and the Christ consciousness. They sponsor all souls seeking union with God, tutoring

them in the fundamental laws governing the cause-effect sequences of their own karma and teaching them how to come to grips with the day-to-day challenges of their individual dharma, one's duty to fulfill the Christ-potential through the sacred labor.

CHAPTER 2:   **The Exchange of the Cosmic Cubes**

1. *The Great White Brotherhood* is a spiritual order of Western saints and Eastern adepts who have reunited with the Spirit of the living God and who comprise the heavenly hosts. They have transcended the cycles of karma and rebirth and have ascended (accelerated) into that higher reality that is the eternal abode of the soul. The ascended masters, united for the highest purposes of the brotherhood of man under the Fatherhood of God, have risen in every age from every culture and religion to inspire creative achievement in education, the arts and sciences, God-government, and the abundant life through the economies of the nations. The word "white" refers not to race but to the aura of white light surrounding their forms. Jesus Christ revealed this heavenly order of saints "robed in white" to his servant John in Revelation. (Rev. 3:4, 5; 6:9–11; 7:9, 13, 14; 19:14)
2. See Matt. 22:10–14.
3. *The causal body* of man surrounds the I AM Presence as the chalice for all good that the individual has elected to qualify in word, thought, and deed since the moment of creation when the blueprint of the soul's identity was sealed in the fiery core of the God Self.
4. *The Fallen One* refers to Lucifer, who was bound on April 16, 1975, and taken to the Court of the Sacred Fire, where he stood trial for a period of ten days. He was sentenced to the second death on April 26, 1975. The "fallen one" could also refer to the seed or descendants of Lucifer or to the archetypal "fallen one," meaning the Antichrist both within and without, personal and planetary.
5. *The thread of contact* is the flow of light between the Spirit of the living God and your soul over the crystal cord. It is the thread of light not only with God but also with all souls ascended in the white light who comprise the Great White Brotherhood. The terms "silver cord" and "crystal cord" are synonymous, being descriptive of man's perceptions of the "umbilical cord" of the soul being tied to and fed by the Spirit.
6. *The altar at Luxor* is located at the retreat of Serapis Bey in the

etheric realm above Luxor, Egypt, called the Ascension Temple. The focus of the ascension flame was carried to Luxor by Serapis Bey, hierarch of the Ascension Temple and chohan of the fourth ray of purity, just before the sinking of Atlantis. Candidates gather at this retreat to receive the tests and initiations leading to the ascension.
7. *The Holy of Holies,* "the most holy place," is the I AM Presence.
8. Matt. 22:1–14.
9. *Summit University* was founded in 1971 by Mark L. Prophet and Elizabeth Clare Prophet under the direction of the ascended masters and was first held at what was the headquarters of The Summit Lighthouse in Santa Barbara, California, at that time. Currently, SU offers online certificate programs in leadership studies, ministerial training courses and in general studies. These are college-level courses available for both credit and audit. Some current courses are: A Survey of the World's Religions, A Spiritual Perspective on the Issues of Our Time, Spiritual Psychology, and many others. See https://SummitUniversity.org/Courses/. Summit University also holds a yearly seminar in July at the Royal Teton Ranch in Montana (available online) and conducts seminars in Europe, South America, and India.
10. *The cube of the microcosm.* On December 2, 1979, Sanat Kumara said, "The mystery of the white cube, my beloved, is that it is the geometrical matrix in Mater wherein the threefold flame of the Trinity is hermetically sealed. The white cube is the symbol of the Mother and of the one who has become the lively stone in the temple of the Mother... the soul enlivened by the indwelling Trinity. Therefore the LORD God has sealed the spark of life within the Matter cube as a veritable sign of the coming of the LORD and of the goal of the path of initiation on the ruby ray—the incarnation of the Word."
11. *The threefold flame* is the flame of the Christ that is the spark of life anchored within the sons and daughters of God and the children of God. It is the sacred trinity of love, wisdom, and power that is the manifestation of the sacred fire. The threefold flame is literally a spark of sacred fire from God's own heart. It is the soul's point of contact with the Supreme Source of all life.
12. Rev. 3:11; 22:7, 12, 20.

CHAPTER 3: **Expect the Unexpected**

1. Following this dictation by Lord Maitreya, the congregation was invited to pass before the messenger to receive the touch of the amethyst egg upon the heart.
2. *The Mediator* describes the universal Christ individualized as the true identity of each one's soul. It is the Real Self of every man, woman, and child to which the soul must rise. The Christ Self is the Mediator between a man and his God, one's advocate before the Father.
3. *Decrees* are a dynamic form of spoken prayer for the purpose of directing God's energy into individual and world conditions to produce constructive change. [See inset "Decrees & the Science of the Spoken Word," pp. 110–15.]
4. Matt. 25:6.
5. *The Keeper of the Scrolls* is the custodian of the archives containing every man's book of life. It is his responsibility to provide the ascended masters and the Karmic Board with the life record of any or all incarnations of an evolving soul about which they may inquire. He is the head of the band of angels known as the angels of record and of all recording angels assigned to the lifewaves evolving in time and space.
6. *The seven last plagues.* Rev. 15:1, 5–8, 16. The release of the vials of the seven last plagues, which was the karma for mankind's misuse of the seven rays, ended in the year 2001.
7. Matt. 5:1–12; Luke 6:20–49.
8. *The Royal Teton Retreat,* congruent with the Teton Range near Jackson Hole, Wyoming, is the principal retreat of the Great White Brotherhood on the North American continent. Confucius is the hierarch of this physical/etheric retreat in the Grand Teton mountain. This retreat is an ancient focus of great light where the seven rays of the Elohim and archangels are enshrined.
9. During the 1975 Christmas season, Lord Maitreya offered a special course in the fires of initiation at the Royal Teton Retreat.
10. *El Morya* is the chohan (Lord) of the first ray, the blue ray of divine power. He tutors souls in gaining self-mastery in the throat chakra and in developing faith, goodwill, leadership, protection, perfection, and surrender to the divine will.
11. *Serapis Bey* is the chohan of the fourth ray and hierarch of the

Ascension Temple at Luxor, Egypt. He is the keeper of the ascension flame and is known as the great disciplinarian. Serapis reviews and trains candidates for the ascension.

12. *Twin flames* are the spirit's masculine or feminine counterpart conceived out of the same white-fire body, the fiery ovoid of the I AM Presence.
13. *The second death* comes as an act of mercy to souls whose karma is so heavy that the suffering that would be entailed in the balancing of their debt to life is considered to be too great for any lifestream to bear. In the process of the second death, the Creator withdraws the energies he has invested in the individualization of the soul, and these energies are drawn into the heart of the sacred fire and returned to the reservoir of God's creative power.
14. *The white-fire core* is the nucleus, the originating focus of Spirit becoming Matter and Matter becoming Spirit. The spiritual Sun behind the physical sun in the center of the universe is not, as it would seem, in back of the physical sun; it is congruent with or superimposed upon it, but in another dimension. Man's own causal body is a miniature replica of the Great Central Sun.
15. *The Tree of Life* (Gen. 3:24) is symbolic of the I AM Presence and causal body of each individual and of the connection of light's children with their immortal Source, as depicted in the Chart of Your Divine Self.
16. John 1:9.
17. *The Great Central Sun Magnet,* the center of flaming love-purity within the Hub, is the focus of the Holy Spirit of God. It energizes the momentums of unity that make all of the universes of God's conscious manifestation an individed whole, an integrated network of galaxies evolving from one dimension to the next.
18. Dan. 3:12–30.
19. *Elemental life* are the beings of earth, air, fire, and water, the nature spirits who are the servants of God and man in the planes of Matter for the establishment and maintenance of the physical plane as the platform for the soul's evolution. Elementals who serve the fire element are called salamanders; those who serve the air element, sylphs; those who serve the water element, undines; those who serve the earth element, gnomes.
20. Mal. 4:2.

21. *The Great Teams of Conquerors* work with the legions of the Elohim Hercules to assist planet Earth.

CHAPTER 4: **The Wooden Begging Bowl**

1. Matt. 26:27.
2. *The love ray,* or the third ray, is the ray of divine love, which conveys the qualities of beauty, creativity, compassion, and love through the heart chakra. Paul the Venetian is the chohan of the third ray and teaches the way of divine love through love in action. He is devoted to beauty as an essential element of the soul. Chamuel and Charity are the archangel and archeia of the third ray. Together with their legions of pink-flame angels, they serve to expand the flame of adoration and divine love within the hearts of men and elementals. The joy of the Christ and the proper use of the creative powers of the Godhead are the forte of their instruction. Heros and Amora are the Elohim of the third ray, and like all other Elohim, are hierarchs in the builders of creation, the first kingdom of cosmic hierarchy. They infuse matter with the cohesive power of the Holy Spirit, the integrating principle of life. By the power of their love, planets are held in their orbits and electrons continue on their appointed rounds.
3. *Aum:* The Sanskrit word *Aum* or *Om* is the sacred syllable of creation, the Word that went forth in the Beginning and from which all other sounds originate. The Aum is spelled *A-u-m,* and each of the letters stands for a component of our divinity. Each letter is intended to be sounded separately. When we blend the Trinity, we intone simply the Aum. Past, present, and future form the Trinity. We are all that we are as past, as present, as future realization of the Aum. In the East, the Hindus refer to the Trinity as Brahma, Vishnu, and Shiva, and in the West it is Father, Son, and Holy Spirit. The concept is the same.
4. *The Electronic Presence* is an exact duplicate of the being of an ascended master, electronic in nature, to the very level of electrons. Therefore Jesus Christ, for example, can place his presence over anyone, over a million people at once, over everyone upon the planet and beyond. And everyone may thereby be standing in the living presence of Jesus Christ.
5. *The universal Christ.* Just as the I AM Presence is the Presence of

God that is individualized for each of us, so the Holy Christ Self is the presence of the universal Christ that is individualized for each of us. "The Christ" is actually a title given to those who have attained oneness with their Higher Self, or Christ Self. That's why Jesus was called "Jesus, the Christ."

CHAPTER 5: **Find Your Way Back to Me**
1. *Adversary.* Both Lucifer and Satan (who have both gone through the second death) and their various lieutenants have been referred to in scripture as the Adversary, the accuser of the brethren, the tempter, the Antichrist, the personification of the carnal mind of mankind, i.e., the planetary dweller-on-the-threshold, Serpent, the beast, the dragon, etc.
2. *First Cause.* In Buddhism the Dharmakaya is one of three "bodies" of the Buddha. It is defined as the Body ("kaya") of Law ("Dharma"), the Body of First Cause, or the Body of Essence, which is one with absolute Reality. The Dharmakaya corresponds to the upper figure in the Chart of Your Divine Self, which is the I AM Presence surrounded by seven concentric spheres of light and consciousness called the causal body. [See inset "The Chart of Your Divine Self," pp. 104–09.]
3. *The Great Divine Director* is a cosmic being whose consciousness has merged with the cosmic cycles of God's divine plan for untold universes of light. His causal body is a giant blue sphere that surrounds the entire planet. Within that sphere, there are grids and forcefields through which the delivery of the judgment shall pass.
4. Matt. 7:16.
5. John the Baptist publicly rebuked Herod because he had married his brother's wife, Herodias, who had abandoned her first husband when Herod divorced his first wife. During a celebration of Herod's birthday, Herodias' daughter, Salome, asked Herod for John's head as a prize. Herod complied, and John's head was presented to Salome on a platter, who then gave it to Herodias. See Matt. 14:3–12; Mark 6:17–29.
6. See Matt. 10:39, 16:25; Mark 8:35; Luke 9:24, 17:33; John 12:25.
7. This dictation by Lord Maitreya was delivered on Sunday, July 2, 1978, during the Freedom class, *Sing a New Song,* held in Pasadena and Camelot, Los Angeles County, California.

8. Before the dictation, the messenger led a meditation entitled, "On the Mother Flame East and West in the Morning Light of the Buddha and the Mother."
9. *The astral plane*, or astral realm, is the frequency of time and space immediately above physical matter, yet below the mental, corresponding to the emotional body of man and the collective unconscious of the race. It is the repository of mankind's thoughts and feelings, conscious and unconscious. Because the astral plane has been muddied by impure thought and feeling, the term "astral" is often used in a negative context to refer to that which is impure or psychic.
10. On July 1, 1978, Saint Germain said: "I have knelt before the altar of Alpha and Omega, and the Father-Mother God has told me, 'Saint Germain, tell the chelas of the ascended masters that from our viewpoint the future of that freedom depends entirely upon their choices made today. We look to no other. For you see, Saint Germain, there are no others who are equipped with the sword of the Spirit to slay the dragons and the beast that would devour the children of God.'"
11. The messenger, Elizabeth Clare Prophet, also referred to as Mother and Guru Ma, gave spiritual counsel to members of the Church and to community members for many years, while also directing them to the guidance of their Higher Self. Although the messenger retired in 1999 and passed on in 2009, those needing her counsel may compose a handwritten letter to her requesting her guidance. The letter would then be burned, and the etheric replica of the letter is taken by angels to Guru Ma. Personal calls may also be made to her requesting her counsel and direction. On March 26, 1997, the messenger said: "It's not necessarily the physical contact with the chela, though I would dearly love to figure out how that physical contact could take place. But it is the contact with the inner Christ that you feel from my inner Christ, my I AM Presence, or my mantle so that all you have to do is think of me and you have my mantle."
12. Ps. 136.
13. *The New Age:* We have entered into the Aquarian age, sometimes called the "New Age," which is one of twelve astrological ages, each about 2,150 years long, which take their names from the signs of

the zodiac. The entire cycle of twelve ages spans about 25,800 years. New ages are related to the "precession of the equinoxes." In astronomy this is the slow rotation of the polar axis of the earth. As the axis so rotates, the point of the spring equinox moves through the signs of the zodiac, denoting which age we are in. No one knows exactly when each age begins or ends, but we do know that we are in the time of transition. Because of the precession, we move through the ages in reverse order. Prior to the age of Pisces, we were in the age of Aries and before that the age of Taurus, and so on. In each age we are destined to assimilate an attribute of God and express the positive aspects of the sign.

14. *Etheric cities* are cities in the etheric plane of planet Earth, the highest vibrating plane of the matter cosmos, i.e., the heaven-world. The etheric frequency and its correspondent plane of consciousness is the repository of the fiery blueprint of the entire physical universe.

CHAPTER 6: **The Initiation of the Law of the One in the Guru-Chela Relationship**

1. See Matt. 5:13.
2. *The Guru-chela relationship* is a spiritual relationship and mentoring tradition that is fundamental to many spiritual traditions. It is the relationship between the Guru (enlightened Teacher) and the chela (the disciple). The Guru-chela relationship is sustained as the ordering of the hierarchy of a cosmos by the law of perfect love.
3. Rev. 14:7.
4. See Rev. 4:4.
5. On May 3, 1977, Gautama Buddha inaugurated a ten-year plan for the turning of the tide of darkness in the earth. He said, "The Lord Buddha has extended to you as the people of God one decade for the turning of the tide... for the spreading abroad of the teachings, for the contacting of hundreds of thousands of souls.... After the decade has passed from this hour, there is no guarantee forthcoming from the Lords of Karma... that the tide can any longer be turned from the fate that has been plotted by the dark ones."
6. Maitreya taught at Summit University during the winter quarter of 1979 at Camelot.
7. Matt. 26:27.

8. *The Lords of Karma,* also known as the Karmic Board, dispense justice to this system of worlds, adjudicating karma, mercy, and judgment on behalf of every lifestream. All souls must pass before the Karmic Board before and after each incarnation on earth, receiving their assignment and karmic allotment for each lifetime beforehand and the review of their performance at its conclusion.

9. *The seven chohans of the rays.* The Tibetan word "chohan" means "lord, master, chief." Each of the seven rays has a chohan who focuses the Christ consciousness of the ray, which is the law of the ray governing its righteous use in man. The seven rays are light emanations of the Godhead, i.e., the seven rays of the white light that emerge through the prism of the Christ consciousness. Each ray focuses a frequency, or color, and has specific qualities. The first ray (blue) focuses faith, will, power, perfection, protection. The second ray (yellow) focuses wisdom, understanding, enlightenment, illumination. The third ray (pink) focuses compassion, kindness, charity, love, beauty. The fourth ray (white) focuses purity, discipline, order, joy. The fifth ray (green) focuses truth, science, healing, music, abundance, vision. The sixth ray (purple and gold) focuses ministration, service, peace, brotherhood. The seventh ray (violet) focuses freedom, mercy, justice, transmutation, forgiveness.

10. Gen. 14:18; Ps. 110:4; Heb. 7:1–10.

11. Teachings on the mysteries of the Holy Grail are available in the book *Mysteries of the Holy Grail* by Archangel Gabriel and in the two MP3 CD set *Mysteries of the Holy Grail,* containing six lectures by Elizabeth Clare Prophet and five dictations by the ascended masters. Available at https://Store.SummitLighthouse.org.

12. In 1977, The Summit Lighthouse purchased the beautiful 218-acre Gillette estate in the Santa Monica Mountains near Malibu, California, and named it "Camelot," in commemoration of King Arthur's mystery school. Headquarters remained at this location through 1986.

13. During the conference, *The Feast of Saint Stephen,* in which this dictation by Lord Maitreya was given, guest speaker Dr. Walter Judd spoke on important geopolitical issues regarding planetary freedom. Many other guest speakers over the years have been

invited to speak during conferences and seminars on issues related to personal and planetary freedom.

14. *Lord of the World* refers to Gautama Buddha, who holds the office of Lord of the World, referred to as "God of the earth" in Rev. 11:4. At inner levels he sustains the threefold flame, the divine spark, for those lifestreams who have lost the direct contact with their I AM Presence and who have made so much negative karma as to be unable to magnetize sufficient light from the Godhead to sustain their souls' physical incarnation on earth. Through a filigree thread of light connecting his heart with the hearts of all God's children, Lord Gautama nourishes the flickering flame of life that ought to burn upon the altar of each heart with a greater magnitude of love, wisdom, and power, fed by each one's own Christ consciousness.

15. *Universities of the Spirit* are spiritual classes in the etheric retreats where souls receive instruction and guidance from members of cosmic hierarchy. At the universities of the Spirit, students can visit each one of the seven chohans of the rays for fourteen consecutive days and then go on to study with the Maha Chohan, who is the director of the seven chohans of the rays. In this way they receive step-by-step instruction on the rays, which enables them to increase their self-mastery. While studying at the retreats, souls also prepare to more efficiently balance their personal karma in daily life.

16. John 1:12.

17. Before this dictation the messenger read from Matthew 5, Mark 10, and John 15.

18. John 18:38.

19. Rev. 19:11.

20. The *"third vision"* is referring to one of the three perilous visions shown to General George Washington by "a mysterious visitor" who appeared to him on an afternoon during the winter of 1777 at Valley Forge. In 1859, a gentleman, Anthony Sherman, then ninety-nine years old, recounted the description of these three visions, or perils, relating to the future destiny of America. The first two perils were the Revolutionary War and the War between the States (the Civil War). In the third vision, Washington saw a dark cloud from Europe, Asia, and Africa envelop America, and he beheld armed hordes engaged in mortal combat with the inhabitants of

America. When a trumpet sounded, a light of ten thousand suns broke the cloud into fragments, and an angel, accompanied by legions of white spirits, joined in the combat until the fragments of the cloud rolled back, leaving the inhabitants victorious. The mysterious visitor then stated: "The most fearful [peril] is the third... passing which the whole world united shall not prevail against her [America]. Let every child of the Republic learn to live for his God, his land and Union."
21. See Acts 7:58–60.

CHAPTER 7: The Garden of Eden

1. Gen. 4.
2. *Satans* (pronounced Seh-tánz): the race of the seed of Satan who long ago rose up against the I AM Race and who have infiltrated every corner of this galaxy and beyond. Jesus Christ pronounced their judgment, concurrent with the final judgment of Satan, in his dictation given February 1, 1982. He said, "I announce to you that the Word has gone forth on Wednesday past, in the very triumph and the hour of the twenty-seventh, for the remanding to the Court of the Sacred Fire of the one you have known for so long as Satan.... Therefore, let it be known that the remanding of Satan to that court, where the Lord Sanat Kumara presides in the presence of the Four and Twenty Elders, has resulted in his final judgment. Therefore rejoice, O ye heavens and the earth! For that power of Satan is bound and that Fallen One is judged and will no more go forth among the inhabitants of this or any other world to tempt them against the Person of the Lord Christ!"
3. Gen. 6:4.
4. Jude 14.
5. Gen. 5:24.
6. Shortly after this dictation by Lord Maitreya, the messenger began to teach on the Book of Enoch. These teachings were later published as *Fallen Angels and the Origins of Evil.*
7. As recorded in *The Forgotten Books of Eden,* the children of Jared were lured down the Holy Mountain of God by the sensual music of the children of Cain. Jared was a descendant of Seth, the son born to Adam and Eve after Cain slew Abel.

8. On January 28, 1979, Mother Mary said: "Let men not trifle with the Word of God! They have sought to trample underfoot the miracles of my sacred heart. These miracles, given unto me by my beloved Son in the name of God the Father, have been the great keys of the history of Western civilization."
9. James 2:10.
10. *The Maha Chohan* is the hierarch of the seven chohans of the rays. His name means "the Great Lord." He embodies the white light of the seven rays and teaches the balance and integration of these rays. The Maha Chohan is also the representative of the Holy Spirit to earth and her evolutions. Because of his pledge to all mankind to keep the flame of life until they are able, he is called the Keeper of the Flame.
11. Heb. 11:6.
12. *Kali* is one of the multiple names of the great Goddess Shakti, one of the spouses of Shiva, Third Person of the Hindu Trinity. She is revered as a great protectress who casts out evil spirits, the way Jesus cast out demons. She represents the fierce aspect of the Divine Mother and is depicted with black skin and wearing a necklace of skulls. Kali's dread appearance symbolizes her boundless power of destruction. It is taught that she shatters the delusions of the ego, destroys ignorance, and preserves order. Her destructive energies are seen as a vehicle of salvation and ultimate transformation. Kali is said to bless and liberate those who yearn for God-realization.
13. *Mighty Astrea* is the feminine complement of the Elohim Purity and works twenty-four hours a day wielding the cosmic circle and sword of blue flame to free the children of the Mother from all that opposes the fulfillment of the divine plan held in the heart of Purity. Astrea personifies the Hindu concept of Kali, "the demon-slayer."
14. *Excalibur* was the name of one or both of the two swords held by King Arthur. The first sword he pulled from a stone, proving that he was the divinely ordained king of England. The second sword he received from the Lady of the Lake [after being mortally wounded in battle]. In some texts, both of Arthur's swords are named Excalibur. In others, only the sword from the Lady of the Lake is called Excalibur. The sword is the symbol of the raised Kundalini. Lanello has said: "The gleaming, silver-white sword

Excalibur, blinding in its presence, signifies the fire of the Mother complete and raised. Thus, it is in truth the appearance of the ascension flame."

15. *Helios and Vesta.* Helios is the God of this solar system and abides in the very heart of the etheric counterpart of the physical sun. With his twin flame, Vesta, he serves to represent the Godhead to those evolving on the planets orbiting the sun. It is their God consciousness that sustains our physical solar system.

16. Kuthumi and Djwal Kul have given tremendous teachings on the studies of the human aura, now published in the book, *The Human Aura: How to Activate and Energize Your Aura and Chakras.* At the time of Jesus' birth, Djwal Kul, Kuthumi, and El Morya were embodied as the three wise men.

17. The seminar was *The Path of Initiation under Maitreya Buddha,* held February 17–19, 1979, at Camelot.

18. *Pearls of Wisdom* are weekly letters of instruction dictated by the ascended masters to their messengers Mark L. Prophet and Elizabeth Clare Prophet for the students of the sacred mysteries throughout the world. The *Pearls of Wisdom* have been published by The Summit Lighthouse continuously since 1958. They contain both fundamental and advanced teachings on cosmic law, with a practical application of spiritual truths to personal and planetary problems. *Pearls of Wisdom* can be ordered through https://www.Summit Lighthouse.org/Pearls-Wisdom or call 1-800-245-5445.

CHAPTER 8: **The Oscillation of Light for the Alignment of Your Soul**

1. Lord Maitreya is referring to the students of Summit University, winter quarter, held at Camelot, which began on January 2, 1979, and ended on March 24, 1979, the date of this dictation. This was the first quarter (class) of Summit University to be sponsored by Lord Maitreya.

2. Matt. 28:20.

3. *Mighty Victory* is a cosmic being whose devotion to the flame of victory for more than a hundred thousand years has given him the authority over that flame through vast reaches of cosmos. His love of the victory of the Christ and the potential victory of those evolving

upon earth was the keynote of his response to Saint Germain's call for cosmic assistance to the earth in the 1930s through the I AM Activity.
4. See note 1.
5. *The twelve hierarchies of the sun* are twelve mandalas of cosmic beings ensouling twelve facets of God's consciousness and hold the pattern of that frequency for the entire cosmos. They are identified by the names of the signs of the zodiac, as they focus their energies to the earth through these constellations.
6. Rev. 21:2, 12–21. The New Jerusalem is also referred to as the City Foursquare.
7. The altar of the Holy Grail refers to the altar within the Chapel of the Holy Grail, the main chapel at the organization's headquarters from 1977 through 1986. This sanctuary was consecrated as the Chapel of the Holy Grail in commemoration of King Arthur's mystery school.
8. *The mantra "Aim"* (pronounced *Ah-eem*) is a bija (one-syllable sound) mantra associated with Saraswati, the Hindu goddess of knowledge, and represents the principle of divine wisdom in nature. Bija is a "seed" mantra, which typically has no literal meaning but provides a connection to specific energies or spiritual principles and assists in accelerating physical, spiritual, and emotional growth and transformation. In yoga practice, bija mantras are chanted while performing poses or during meditation in order to focus the yogi's concentration on a single purpose and/or to still the mind.
9. *The Goddess of Light,* also known as Amerissis, is a powerful being who ensouls the quality of light. It has been written that she was embodied in South America thousands of years ago and had such great attainment that she was able to maintain life in one body for more than five hundred years. It was after she had lived for five hundred years that her lower form was imprisoned in the body of a fish because in an unguarded moment she was congratulating herself on all of her attainments. She was therefore vulnerable to black magicians, who intended to bring about her destruction. For another three hundred years she served her fellowman from behind a counter and wore full-length skirts so no one would be aware of

her condition. While she continued to serve humanity, the constant prayer she uttered was "Light, light, light, expand! Light expand! Light expand! Light expand, expand, expand!" Her prayerful command reached such a crescendo that by edict of the Lords of Karma the scales of bondage parted and she gazed upon the perfect body now restored by light. Amerissis made her ascension at the close of that embodiment. The etheric retreat of Amerissis, the Shrine of Glory, is located in the Andes Mountains in South America.
10. *The Evil One* is also called the Devil. Lucifer first *d*eified *Evil* and then became the personification, or personhood, of that *d*eified *e*nergy *veil.*
11. See Ps. 111:10; Prov. 9:10.
12. Gen. 3:15; Rev. 12:17.

CHAPTER 9: **A Meditation on the Glorious Mission of Our Brotherhood**

1. Lord Maitreya maintains an etheric retreat in the Himalayas, where he focuses the flame of initiation. The retreat is composed of white marble and includes a vast marble chapel. On April 9, 1971, he said: "I extend to you evolving upon this planetary body, from the Far East, from our etheric home of light, a welcome to visit us often in your finer bodies while your physical bodies sleep. And then let your souls awaken within our retreat that you may have the knowledge and the desire and the beautiful concepts we desire to convey to you."
2. On November 25, 1979, Sanat Kumara delivered a dictation in which he explained the meaning of the words, "Drink me while I AM drinking thee." "This is the sign of the receiving and the giving of the waters of the Word—the true teachings of Christ." He said, "In the inner chamber, called the Upper Room, there is an inscription that is written: *Drink Me While I AM Drinking Thee.* Those who are received of the Lord on the path of the ruby ray to be partakers of his body and his blood are taught the meaning of this command of the Great Initiator [Lord Maitreya], which has become the mantra of Mother and Maitreya singing in the hearts of the saints."
3. *Himalaya* is the Manu of the fourth root race. He is also the hierarch of the etheric Retreat of the Blue Lotus in the Himalayan mountains.

The gentle radiance of Himalaya can be felt throughout the East as a tangible presence, drawing the pilgrims of all nations into a divine awareness of the flame of the blue lotus.

4. *Babaji* is an unascended master of the Himalayas. He has become well-known in the West through the writings of Paramahansa Yogananda. Babaji has chosen to forgo the ascension by reason of the bodhisattva ideal, which means that he desires to remain on earth until everyone has won their freedom.

5. *Manu.* Sanskrit for the progenitor and lawgiver of the evolutions of God on earth. The Manu and his divine complement are ascended twin flames assigned by the Father-Mother God to sponsor and ensoul the Christic image for a certain evolution or lifewave that is known as a root race—souls who embody as a group and have a unique archetypal pattern, divine plan, and mission to fulfill on earth. According to esoteric tradition, there are seven primary aggregations of souls, i.e., the first to the seventh root races. (Also see note 14, this chapter.)

6. *Beloved Chananda,* chief of the Indian Council of the Great White Brotherhood, gave a dictation immediately preceding this one by Lord Maitreya. Chananda announced the intention of the Indian Council and the Darjeeling Council to open an ashram to the World Mother in India and establish a figure-eight flow between East and West. In the summer of 1980, the messenger opened the ashram in New Delhi.

7. The messenger traveled to India from April 11 to April 20, 1980. On April 17, the Maha Chohan, through the messenger, dedicated the Ashram of the World Mother in New Delhi.

8. "The ascended messenger" is referring to Mark L. Prophet, who made his transition and ascension on February 26, 1973. "The chair" refers to one of two chairs that were present on the altar of the Chapel of the Holy Grail at Camelot at the time of this dictation. The two chairs, still present on the altar at the Church's headquarters in Corwin Springs, Montana, represent the two messengers of the Great White Brotherhood and the two witnesses spoken of in Revelation 11:3–14.

9. Lord Maitreya is referring to the last word spoken at this conference, *Harpstrings of Lemuria.*

10. *The Everlasting Gospel.* The ascended masters have taught that the Everlasting Gospel is the composite of all of the teachings of the Great White Brotherhood delivered by the two witnesses in many forms. Revelation 14:6 reads: "And I saw another angel fly in the midst of heaven, having the everlasting gospel to preach unto them that dwell on the earth, and to every nation, and kindred, and tongue, and people." The messenger has explained that the Everlasting Gospel is also a thoughtform and a matrix of the mind of God, a sphere of yellow that surrounds the earth, imparting to all people the sense of the universality of religion. The nine volumes of the Climb the Highest Mountain series have been spoken of as a key element of the Everlasting Gospel.
11. *The eighth ray* is the ray of integration. It is a transition ray between the seven rays, which are for the mastery in the planes of matter of the Christ consciousness, and the five secret rays, which are within the white-fire core of being. The five secret rays represent a going within for the mastery of God, whereas the seven outer rays represent the coming without and the mastery of the environment. These cycles are a pattern of the going within and the coming out—the Eastern teachings, going within; the Western teachings, going without.
12. Rev. 5:1–5.
13. *The dweller-on-the-threshold* is a term sometimes used to designate the anti-self, the not-self, the synthetic self, the antithesis of the Real Self, the conglomerate of the self-created ego, ill-conceived through the inordinate use of the gift of free will, consisting of the carnal mind and a constellation of misqualified energies, forcefields, focuses, animal magnetism comprising the subconscious mind.
14. *The fourth and fifth root races.* Root races are souls who embody as a group, having a unique archetypal pattern, divine plan, and mission to fulfill on earth. The first three root races ascended aeons ago during earth's golden ages. During the fourth root race, the fall of man took place under the influence of the fallen angels on earth, and this race was followed by the fifth root race, which was also influenced by the fallen ones. These races as a whole have not ascended and are still in embodiment on earth, though some individuals from among these root races have likely ascended. The sixth root race took incarnation approximately two thousand years ago in support of the mission of Jesus. Some souls of the sixth root race

have not yet embodied. The seventh root race is destined to embody in South America during the current age of Aquarius, when the conditions on earth have improved enough to receive these souls. Each of these races is meant to embody the qualities of one of the seven rays. (See note 5.)

15. *Afra* was the first member of the black race to make his ascension. Long ago he offered name and fame to God to sponsor a vast continent and a mighty people. When he ascended, he asked to be called simply "a brother" (*frater* in Latin), hence the name Afra. The continent of Africa takes its name from Afra, and he is the patron of Africa and of the black race.

16. *Zadkiel and Holy Amethyst* are the archangels of the seventh ray, Arcturus and Victoria are the Elohim of the seventh ray. Kuan Yin also serves on the seventh ray and is revered in Buddhism as the compassionate Saviouress, the Bodhisattva of Mercy.

17. *Surya and Cuzco.* Surya is a cosmic being from Sirius, whose flame is an intense blue tinged with white. He wields the tremendous power of the God Star, Sirius on behalf of the evolutions of earth. The God Star, Sirius (known as the "Dog Star") is the seat of God-government in this sector of our galaxy. Surya is traditionally depicted seated on a lotus in a chariot of gold drawn by seven horses or by a single horse with seven heads. He holds the balance for natural forces in the earth and is assisted by the ascended master Cuzco, disciple of Surya and director of his retreat of God's will near Suva, the Sacred Retreat of the Blue Flame.

CHAPTER 10: Love of the Person and the Law of the Word: God and My Right

1. Continuing the sponsorship of Summit University by the Karmic Board, the ascended lady master Portia, also called the Goddess of Justice or the Goddess of Opportunity and who is the twin flame of Saint Germain, presided at Summit University fall quarter 1980.

2. In Greek mythology, Daedalus and his son Icarus attempted to escape the wrath of King Minos by fastening wings to their bodies with wax and taking to the air. Disobeying his father's instructions, Icarus flew too close to the sun, the wax melted, and the boy fell into the sea and drowned.

3. Richard I of England, surnamed *Cour de Lion,* "the Lion Hearted," at the Battle of Gisors in 1198, chose this phrase, *Dieu et mon droit* (God and my right) as his parole, or battle word, meaning that he was not the vassal of France but owed his royalty to God alone. He won a great victory, in honor of which the phrase was instated as the motto of the Royal Arms of England.
4. Isa. 7:14; Matt. 1:23.
5. *The Impersonal Personality.* Saint Germain has spoken of the four aspects of God: The Father as an Impersonal Impersonality, of God the Son as an Impersonal Personality, of God the Mother as a Personal Personality, and the Holy Spirit as a Personal Impersonality. The Impersonal Impersonality of God is a Law. It is a principle. It is a Spirit. It is the I AM THAT I AM, the Father Principle, the Supreme Lawgiver seen in the religion of the patriarchs and prophets of ancient Israel. The Impersonal Personality of God is the Son, the Christ Self of each one of us. The Impersonal Personality is the Word incarnate, the mind of God become the mind of Christ. In the figure of Jesus the Christ we see the Impersonal Personality.
6. John 5:17.
7. See Rev. 2:7.
8. John 5:14; 8:11.
9. *The Monad,* or *Divine Monad,* consists of the I AM Presence surrounded by the spheres (color rings) of light that make up the body of First Cause, or causal body. These spheres are the many mansions of the Father's house where we lay up for ourselves "treasures in heaven." (Matt. 6:20) Also see the inset "The Chart of Your Divine Self, pp. 104–09.

CHAPTER 11: **The Dilemma of the Soul in the Evolutionary Cosmos**

1. Serapis Bey gave a dictation just prior to this dictation by Lord Maitreya, in which he said: "Blessed hearts, unless love had the built-in self-defense of its own self-preservation, the fallen ones would long ago have swallowed it up. But it was not to be. And it could not be. And it cannot. For you see, the ruby ray itself is the essential, I say, *essential* element of love whereby all anti-love, as hatred, is turned in upon itself and self-consumed. Therefore, by the

right hand of Serapis I send the ruby ray as radiating light, as the corona of this sphere of our causal body, even the causal body of the entire Spirit of the Great White Brotherhood!... Now I release the ruby ray for all who would have it from my heart—for the melting down of hardness of heart, for the melting down of barriers and shells behind which you have hidden because you yourselves have felt that same rejection. This is their desire to stop you from loving purely, wholly, freely, fully!"
2. Throughout the years the messengers have delivered many lectures and presentations on current events, including government, education, and the economy, explaining and exposing how these areas of life have been manipulated by the forces of darkness on earth, how their strategies can be overturned, and how society and government can be raised up by invoking the light.
3. Archangel Gabriel has spoken about the mysteries of life and death, this world and the next, and the nature of an ages-old conspiracy to dominate the minds and souls and hearts of the lifewaves not only of planet Earth but of this and other systems of worlds. He was eyewitness to the antediluvian epochs, and he speaks to us of the books of our father Enoch, vividly interpreting the battle of Light and Darkness. In his book *Mysteries of the Holy Grail* (see chapter 6, note 11), Gabriel has given his teaching concerning the knowledge of relative good and evil and how it was transmitted to our first earthly parents by fallen angels who conspired to tear the veil of innocence from Adam and Eve so that they might no longer see the Lord God face-to-face, and so that their progeny would be led astray for thousands of years.
4. In the dictation by Serapis Bey given prior to this dictation, he said: "Blessed ones, in this fourteen-month cycle abuilding from the spiral of our heart, there is the opportunity for you to enter a path of initiation whereby love is perfected in love.... It is a new appreciation of love that the purity of white fire can give to you in this fourteen-month of the bearing of the cosmic cross of white fire with the ruby ray—if you will be conscious that that is the message of this path of initiation.... I come to release the fourteen-month spiral as I place it as a nucleus in your heart. But I come to warn you, as I have warned you with each of the prior releases, that the

continuing intensity of ascension's fire propelling out the cycles of the causal body will give you greater and greater initiations—more to conquer both of Reality and of unreality."

5. *The Dark Cycle* of the return of mankind's karma began on April 23, 1969. It is a period when mankind's misqualified energy (i.e., their returning negative karma), held in abeyance for centuries under the great mercy of the Law, is released according to the cycles of the initiations of the solar hierarchies for balance in this period of transition into the Aquarian age. April 23, 1980, commenced the twelfth year of the Dark Cycle (initiation under the hierarchy of Sagittarius and their God consciousness of victory). On April 23, 1981, the initiations of the karmic return continued to mount under the hierarchy of Capricorn. The Dark Cycle concluded on April 22, 2002.

6. On April 1, 1981, Alpha gave a dictation entitled, "The Time Is Short."

7. *The Nephilim* [Heb. "those who fell" or "those who were cast down"; from the Semitic root *naphal* "to fall"] are a biblical race of giants or demigods, referred to in Genesis 6:4. The Greek Septuagint, a late translation of the Hebrew scriptures, rendered the word Nephilim as "giants." ("There were giants in the earth in those days") Author Zecharia Sitchin concludes from his study of ancient Sumerian texts that the Nephilim were an extraterrestrial race who "fell" to earth (landed) in spacecraft 450,000 years ago. The term is also used to describe the fallen angels who were cast out of heaven into the earth. (Rev. 12:7–9)

8. *Mechanization man.* In the long millennia since darkness first came upon the planet, earth has been host to many different evolutions, and not all of these evolutions descended from God. Jesus makes this clear in the Gospels when he says of the Pharisees, "You are of your father, the devil. I am from above; you are from beneath." Jesus left a record of these different evolutions in the parable of the tares and the wheat. He explained to his disciples that the good seed were the children of God and that the tares were sown by the enemy, the devil, and these were the seed, the offspring of the evil one.

9. *The God Star, Sirius* (known as the "Dog Star") is the seat of God-government in this sector of our galaxy. It is held by astronomers

to be a binary star of the constellation Canis Major and is the brightest star in the heavens. Sirius was known to the ancients as the "Royal One." Its name is generally thought to be derived from the Greek word for "sparkling" or "scorching." The name in Arabic, *Al Shi'ra,* is so similar to its name in Egyptian, Persian, Greek and other languages that one nineteenth-century astronomer thought they might have had a common ancient source, possibly the Sanskrit *Surya,* meaning "the Shining One," "the Sun." In Hindu lore and religion, Surya is the sun or sun god.

10. *The Inner Retreat* is a physical outpost of the Great White Brotherhood at the Royal Teton Ranch in the Paradise Valley of southwestern Montana. It is the international headquarters of The Summit Lighthouse and Church Universal and Triumphant. The land of the Inner Retreat and particularly the Heart of the Inner Retreat, a secluded mountain meadow at an elevation of six thousand feet, is consecrated ground and is considered to be a sacred or holy land. The Inner Retreat is partially in the etheric octave, and numerous ascended masters have spoken of walking this hallowed ground. It is the place where the soul meets or encounters the Real Self, the guru in the form of the messengers and the ascended masters, particularly Lord Maitreya.

11. *The cosmic clock* is the science of charting the cycles of the soul's karma and initiations on the twelve lines of the clock under the twelve hierarchies of the Great Central Sun. It was taught by Mother Mary to Mark L. Prophet and Elizabeth Clare Prophet for sons and daughters of God returning to the Law of the One and their point of origin beyond the worlds of form and lesser causation. It is an inner astrology whereby we can chart the cycles of our karma and be the master of our fate, our cycles, and our destiny. It also allows us to chart the cycles of our dharma and to fulfill our reason for being. As the wheel of the cosmic clock turns day by day and we experience the cycles of our tests and initiations in life, an awareness of this science can help us pass these tests. The book by Elizabeth Clare Prophet *Predict Your Future: Understand the Cycles of the Cosmic Clock* gives detailed teaching on this subject. Available at https://Store.SummitLighthouse.org.

12. The law of the seven and the seven steps means mastering the seven

rays in each one of the seven chakras. Djwal Kul teaches that "it is the requirement of the initiation of the buddhic consciousness that you fulfill the law of the seven chakras in each of the planes of God's consciousness. Therefore, once you have gained the mastery of the heart chakra, that mastery must be transferred to each of the other chakras. This, then, will be the fulfillment of the seven rays as the mastery of the heart chakra is transferred to the others." Gautama admonishes us to attain God-mastery in the law of the seven rays. Lanello teaches that "the return to God is a pathway walked through the initiations of the seven sacraments. Though the first is given at baptism at birth, all of these seven continue throughout life, day by day fulfilling the law of the seven rays, which the seven sacraments represent—and the seven chakras." There are seven steps to precipitation, and these are outlined in the Lord's Prayer as seven commands of the Word, beginning with "Hallowed be thy name," and ending with "For thine is the kingdom and the power and the glory forever." These seven commands follow the seven rays of the Holy Spirit that come out of the nucleus of the Christ consciousness.

13. *Maitreya: Ma*—the universal sound intoning the Mother flame; *i*—the I or Eye signifying the identity of the Guru as the individualization of the Mother flame; *t*—the sign of the cross signifying the path of initiation of each disciple of the Cosmic Christ; *rey*—the ray of the Mother's light manifesting in you; *a*—as you are the seed of Alpha (the alpha particle).

CHAPTER 12: **The Visitation of the Stars**

1. *Keepers of the Flame* refers to members of the Keepers of the Flame Fraternity, founded in 1961 by Saint Germain; an organization of ascended masters and their chelas who vow to keep the flame of life on earth and support the activities of the Great White Brotherhood in the establishment of their community and mystery school and in the dissemination of their teachings. Keepers of the Flame receive graded lessons in cosmic law dictated by the ascended masters to their messengers Mark L. Prophet and Elizabeth Clare Prophet.

2. Serapis Bey gave a dictation just prior to this dictation by Lord Maitreya, in which he said: "Blessed ones, in this fourteen-month

spire abuilding from the spiral of our heart, there is the opportunity for you to enter a path of initiation whereby love is perfected in love. There is a room at Luxor where this inscription is seen above the door: 'Love Is Perfected in Love.' It is the name of a course as a path that is set.... It is a new appreciation of love that the purity of white fire can give to you in this fourteen-month bearing of the cosmic cross of white fire with the ruby ray—if you will be conscious that that is the message of this path of initiation. Love can be perfected in love only when you start with perfect love.... Go and find it in the song of the bird at dawn. Go and find it in the dewdrop on the rose. Find it as you meditate upon nature's floral offerings. Find perfect love in the heart of a loved one as you pass universes of manifestation and go straight as an arrow to the God who dwells in that heart. It is not so hard to find perfect love. Look for it in a mother's smile, in the tenderness of father, the sweetness of a child's prayer at eventide, or the rejoicing in the fields of Maytime. Why, perfect love is all around you."

3. Rev. 19:7.
4. Dan. 12:2, 3.
5. See chapter 6, note 5.
6. *The test of the ten* is the test of selflessness, which always involves the test of the emotions and of the God-control of those emotions through the Divine Ego.
7. On April 18, 1981, the day before this dictation by Lord Maitreya, Gautama Buddha gave a dictation entitled, "The Arcing of the Flame of Shamballa to the Inner Retreat," in which he said: "Now therefore, my beloved, in this hour I contemplate—note it well—the arcing of the flame of Shamballa to the Inner Retreat as the Western abode of the Buddhas and the bodhisattvas and the bodhisattvas-to-be who are the devotees of the Mother light.... Our longing is to be one in the Inner Retreat. Our longing is to lower into physical dimensions all that is prepared. For in the physical octave the light shineth, the light is come. In the physical octave we would celebrate the light of the Central Sun. Only thus shall the transformation of worlds occur. Only thus shall the cycles end—and the cycles begin!"
8. *The antahkarana of life* is the net of light spanning Spirit and Matter,

connecting and sensitizing the whole of creation within itself and to the heart of God.

CHAPTER 13: **The Dispensation of the Righteous Branch**

1. Jer. 23:5; 33:15; Zech. 3:8; 6:12.
2. The sermon given by the messenger prior to this dictation, which was taken from Jeremiah 30–31and 33, was on the subject of the Lord's comfort and promise of healing to the children of Israel.
3. The messenger commented on Jeremiah 31:17: "And there is hope in thine end, saith the LORD, that thy children shall come again to their own border." Mrs. Prophet said, "Thy children, thy children's children, thy very own soul shall reincarnate to their own border of the land of the union [America]."
4. Exod. 28:36–38; 39:30, 31; Isa. 23:18; Jer. 2:3; Zech. 14:20, 21.
5. Rev. 21:2, 10–27.
6. See Jer. 23:5.
7. Num. 18; Deut. 18:1–8.
8. The Bethel Stone (*bethel* meaning "the house of God"), is the stone upon which Jacob rested his head the night he dreamed of the heavenly ladder. (Gen. 28:10–22) In the sermon prior to the dictation, the messenger explained that according to tradition Jeremiah took the Bethel Stone with him when he journeyed to Ireland and that it became the coronation stone upon which the kings of the House of David were crowned. Some scholars believe it to be the Stone of Scone, which now rests under the coronation chair in Westminster Abbey.
9. The outer focus of Shamballa is referring to the Inner Retreat, which is described in chapter 12, note 7. Shamballa, the original retreat of Sanat Kumara, is on the etheric plane over the Gobi Desert.
10. On August 3, 1980, Archangel Gabriel said: "I preach the Word of the Revolution of the Woman Clothed with the Sun and I make it the revolution of every woman who is of God, who is born out of the light of Alpha and Omega. And this Revolution for the '80s is not to be taken [up] nor will it be allowed by the fallen ones. They will not take this revolution to their own and confute and confound the Word of God!" On September 14, 1980, Elizabeth Clare Prophet said: "The whole point of this [Woman's Revolution of the '80s] is

taking the science of the spoken Word and applying it to the issues that confront us, not only as women but in the realization that we are mothers of civilization and that the Mother flame in men and women must be raised up as the sacred fire that can be directed through the spoken Word to solve the problems of the government, the economy, and education."

11. Rev. 19:11–21.
12. Rev. 12.
13. In Lord Maitreya's statement "Let the unrighteous leader be cast down," he may be referring to a specific or archetypical leader who does not bear the mantle of the Christ, as King David of Israel did. In a lecture given just prior to this dictation by Lord Maitreya, the messenger spoke of David as being the archetype of the Christ incarnate. She read from the Book of Jeremiah 30:21 and paraphrased this verse by saying, "I will raise out of their very midst the sons of God to be their leaders, and no more shall their leaders come from the false gods and the fallen ones." Following her reading of Jeremiah 33:15 and 16, she said, "Now we hear that the name of the one who is the leader is called The Lord Our Righteousness, who is the Christ in the individual. But we also hear that the community of the Holy Spirit, even the New Jerusalem, shall be called The Lord Our Righteousness because collectively that people have raised up the perfect light." The messenger then read Jeremiah 33:17 and said, "This is the promise that from that hour unto the present, there has always been one in incarnation who has been the bearer of the light, holding the key to the incarnation of God."
14. A lecture tour titled "Woman's Revolution of the '80s" was held by staff women of The Summit Lighthouse in cities across America. It was first requested by the ascended master Portia in July of 1980, who said: "Those who represent us in the feminine ray, those who are the gentle but powerful women in our midst, they must also, in their representation of our flame, hold meetings with women all over this country, showing them how they can raise up the light, and in so doing restore the holy family and give vitality to their communities."

CHAPTER 14:   **The Living Book**

1. *The Passion Week* is the week beginning on Palm Sunday and ending on Easter Sunday, commemorating the entrance of Jesus into Jerusalem, his teaching in the temple, the Last Supper, Jesus' arrest in the Garden of Gethsemane, his trial before Annas, Caiaphas and the Sanhedrin, Herod Antipas, and Pontius Pilate, the stations on the road to Golgotha and his crucifixion and resurrection. These scenarios, as recorded in the four gospels, portray the tests, trials, and initiations that all must pass through on the path of initiation leading to the ascension.
2. *The One Sent* refers to the one who is sent by the lineage of the Great White Brotherhood as an emissary, such as an avatar (divine incarnation) or messenger. The One Sent can also mean each one's individual Holy Christ Self.
3. *The woman* refers to the Divine Mother travailing to give birth to the universal, planetary, and individual Christ consciousness ("a man child"). See Rev. 12:1, 2, 5.
4. John 16:33.
5. *Ephraim's sons* are the descendants or seed of Ephraim, one of the sons of the Patriarch Joseph, who today are reincarnated in America. For Old Testament references, see Gen. 50:23; Num. 26:35–37; I Chron. 7:20–27.
6. In a dictation of January 2, 1982, the Elohim Purity and Astrea referred to "the circle of cosmic fire" in their comments on the affirmative response of the students, "Let their voice [of Elohim] be heard," saying: "This agreement twixt heaven and earth is the completing of the circle of cosmic fire." Purity envisioned "a worldwide movement of lightbearers, of all members of the I AM Race, whose thread of contact through the Mother is with the heart of Gautama Buddha at Shamballa and in the heart of the Inner Retreat."
7. During the decade of the 1980s and continuing, various building projects have taken place at the Inner Retreat to provide housing, office space, and a main chapel. The current main chapel was established in a barn-like structure and now named King Arthur's Court. In 1999–2000, renovations were begun on King Arthur's Court and completed in 2008, transforming the original structure

into a beautiful chapel. In 2005, ground was broken for construction of a new office building, which was completed in April of 2006. For more information, see chapter 11, note 10.
8. See II Cor. 5:17.
9. John 9:39.
10. John 12:23.
11. See Elizabeth Clare Prophet, *Fallen Angels and the Origins of Evil: Why Church Fathers Suppressed the Book of Enoch and Its Startling Revelations*, "The Book of the Secrets of Enoch," pp. 409–67. Available at https://Store.SummitLighthouse.org.
12. The teachings of Enoch were delivered to the two witnesses (Rev. 11:3), Mark L. Prophet and Elizabeth Clare Prophet. "The Book of Enoch" is published in its entirety in *Fallen Angels and the Origins of Evil*.
13. The teachings of Enoch, including the Secrets of Enoch, are on an MP3 disc entitled *Enoch's Rosary*, which includes a reading from "The Book of the Secrets of Enoch" and other apocryphal works, a lecture by Mark L. Prophet, four dictations from the ascended master Enoch, songs, invocations, and mantras. Available at https://Store.SummitLighthouse.org.
14. The Easter conference, *Easter Conclave 1982*, was held April 7–11, 1982, at Camelot.

CHAPTER 15: **In the Heart of the One Sent**

1. *Some say I embodied.* Benjamin Crème (1922–2016), British author-lecturer and self-proclaimed representative of Lord Maitreya, announced on May 14, 1982, in Los Angeles, that the Cosmic Christ had entered the modern world and had been living in a Pakistani community in southeast London since July 19, 1977. According to Crème, the master would identify himself within two weeks in an international radio and television broadcast, in which he would communicate telepathically with all people on earth in their own language. Maitreya failed to appear and identify himself, and many of Crème's followers became disillusioned.
2. *Pictured in the hand of the Mother.* Maitreya is referring to the painting by Ray Brown depicting the messenger clad in a white dress and blue mantle and holding a sword in her right hand and

the book of the Law in the other hand; a flying eagle hovers above the messenger. This painting hangs on the back wall of King Arthur's Court, the chapel at the Inner Retreat. Sanat Kumara commissioned, unveiled, and blessed this painting, saying: "Receive it as an image of yourself—yourself as Mother, yourself as part of the one body of God. . . . It is a painting of the messenger; it is also a painting of myself. . . . I appear in the person of the eagle, in the person of the Great Causal Body. . . . In this image you see a forerunner of the intense action of the physical stepping through the veil not only of the ascended masters but also of your own Christ Self."

3. *Confucius and Lord Lanto* focus the flame of illumination at the Royal Teton Retreat, where they, with Saint Germain, conduct their universities of the Spirit. The ascended master Confucius is the hierarch of the Royal Teton Retreat and serves on the second ray of divine wisdom. He succeeded Lord Lanto, chohan of the second ray, as hierarch of this retreat on July 3, 1958.
4. Mark 1:2; Luke 7:27.
5. Luke 17:21.
6. John 9:4.

MAITREYA MYSTERY SCHOOL SERIES
Volume 1

Teachings from the Mystery School
The Maitreya Discourses

Come and Find Me...

Welcome to the Mystery School of Lord Maitreya—the Buddha of mercy, love and compassion.

Two thousand years ago, Maitreya sent forth the call to his disciple, Jesus, to come and find him. And so Jesus set out for the Himalayas to find the Father, Maitreya, and to receive the teachings that would be the key to an age. Now, once again, Maitreya sends forth the call. Are you one of these fiery spirits that Maitreya Buddha is calling?

376 PP   ISBN 978-1-60988-379-9

Jesus tells us that the Mystery School of Lord Maitreya is "the open door of the coming of the golden age. This is the open door of the pathway of East and West, of the bodhisattvas and the disciples.... For once again it may be said that Maitreya is physically present, not as it was in the first Eden but by the extension of ourselves in form through the messenger and the Keepers of the Flame."

Soon after the announcement of the opening of his Mystery School, Lord Maitreya began a series of profound discourses. He asked us to search these teachings and to discover in them the keys to this Age of Maitreya.

In this book you will find those keys to anchoring the consciousness of the Cosmic Christ in your life. Maitreya beckons: "Come and Find Me."

Welcome to the adventure of the ages.

Teachings of the Cosmic Christ   Volume 1
Restoring the Thread of Contact

Teachings from the Mystery School. In an ancient past—now only recalled in a Biblical account that many think of as legend—man and woman walked and talked with God in the garden of an earthly paradise.

Then came the Fall. We no longer saw the Guru face-to-face. The world became our teacher—the lessons often hard.

Now comes Maitreya—Guru of old. He would open the door of the ancient mystery school once more. But there are requirements to be met before we are ready to enter.

Maitreya would show us the way. The first step: to reestablish the thread of contact with the Guru—and with our own Real Self.

Enter the path of the Cosmic Christ. Regain the Edenic consciousness. Find your way back Home.

376 PP   ISBN 978-1-60988-379-9

Maitreya on Initiation
The Coming Buddha Who Has Come

Maitreya, the Coming Buddha, the Future Buddha, plays many roles in the various Buddhist traditions throughout the Far East.

Maitreya on Initiation is a compilation of Elizabeth Clare Prophet's lectures and writings on Maitreya throughout the years. Also included are five messages on initiation from the Great Initiator himself.

246 PP   ISBN 978-1-932890-04-4

The Opening of the Seventh Seal

Sanat Kumara on the Path of the Ruby Ray

In this book Sanat Kumara, spoken about as the "Ancient of Days" in the Bible and as "Dipamkara" in the Buddhist tradition, delivers profound teachings on the path of initiation. Insights are given into mystical passages from the Book of Revelation, the Book of Ezekiel and the path of initiation which Sanat Kumara transfers to us through the Lord Maitreya.

This is your textbook for opening the seven spheres of cosmic consciousness—and keys to re-creating your soul in the likeness of God.

426 PP   ISBN 978-0-922729-68-5

The Masters and Their Retreats

The great lights who have come out of all the world's spiritual traditions and graduated from earth's schoolroom have become widely known as masters. They demonstrate that in the world of Spirit, there is no division of race, religion or philosophy—there is simply oneness, ineffable sweetness and love. What is not so widely known is that these great masters have retreats—temples and cities of light in the heaven world—where we can go in spiritual meditation and while our bodies sleep at night. In this comprehensive work, Mark L. Prophet and Elizabeth Clare Prophet talk about these great masters, the stories of their lives and their magnificent spiritual retreats.

560 PP   ISBN 978-0-9720402-4-2

About The Summit Lighthouse

The Summit Lighthouse is an internationally recognized spiritual center for the advancement of inner awakening. Our international organization is a global family that is inspired, guided, and sponsored by those known as the ascended masters.

The ascended masters are the most beloved and trusted transcendent beings guiding our planet's material and spiritual evolution. Most of the world's religions are currently based on the revelations of one or more of these masters before their ascension. We openly embrace spiritual seekers from all paths of light including the mystical traditions of the world's religions.

The ascended masters and their messengers have given us over fifteen thousand hours of invaluable inner wisdom and insightful instruction, and they have provided the means for our direct initiation into higher consciousness.

For the ascended masters . . . no subject is off limits! Their teachings contain amazing truths and awesome answers on spirituality, alchemy, astrology, sacred geometry, spiritual science, karma, reincarnation, ascension, archangels (and fallen angels), and even those issues that are considered taboo or "out of this world."

Primary Goals of the Teachings of the Ascended Masters

The ascended masters challenge us daily to be bold, to dare to be who we truly are, and to face adversity with courage, patience, perseverance, honesty, integrity, inner love, discipline, and discernment—all for a greater sense of inner peace, fearlessness, stillness and silence, harmony, self-mastery, compassion, and wisdom.

These teachings help our souls get back to the origin of their individualized inner source of True Self Love—the Higher Self, or I AM Presence. Our point of contact with our Higher Self is the "Spark of Life" or "Sacred Fire of the Heart," the place where our consciousness expresses its true divine nature of unconditional love and happiness, universal oneness, and an authentic desire to serve others.

How Our Teachings Came into Being

Our teachings were all released through highly trained and trusted messengers, Mark L. Prophet and Elizabeth Clare Prophet. Mark was contacted by the ascended master El Morya at the age of eighteen and received training from him for many years before he was instructed to establish The Summit Lighthouse in 1958 in Washington, D.C.

With his ascension in 1973, Mark passed the torch for the mission to his gifted wife, Elizabeth Clare Prophet, who continued her service until her retirement in 1999.

The dictations of the ascended masters were regularly given in public. The ascended masters also inspired thousands of lectures delivered by the messengers. The content of the dictations are, by most human standards, beyond the mind's ability to construct in real time. They carry very powerful frequencies of light, awakening us to the highest truths we've ever experienced.

We leave it up to you to decide the value for yourself.

Moving toward Your Victory

No matter what path of light you are on, spiritual freedom is attained using tools that have been passed down in wisdom teachings through the millennia: meditation, selfless service, devotional music, prayer, mantra, and the science of the spoken Word. The masters bring an accelerated understanding of these principles, especially suited for the challenges of the modern world, including dynamic decree work and the use of the violet flame.

Next Steps

We are genuinely excited to meet you on the Path and hope you are too. We extend a warm welcome from everyone at The Summit Lighthouse, and we invite you to explore the teachings of the ascended masters at **www.SummitLighthouse.org.** Check out our free online lessons and hundreds of articles on a wide range of spiritual subjects. Browse through our online bookstore. And if you would rather talk to someone in person, please feel free to contact us today!

The Summit Lighthouse®
63 Summit Way
Gardiner, Montana 59030 USA
1-800-245-5445 / 406-848-9500
Se habla español.
info@SummitUniversityPress.com
SummitLighthouse.org

ELIZABETH CLARE PROPHET is a world-renowned author, spiritual teacher, and pioneer in practical spirituality. Her groundbreaking books have been published in more than thirty languages and over three million copies have been sold worldwide.

For more information about Elizabeth Clare Prophet's work, including her Pocket Guides to Practical Spirituality and her series on the Lost Teachings of Jesus and the Mystical Paths of the World's Religions, visit SummitUniversityPress.com.

Printed in the USA
CPSIA information can be obtained
at www.ICGtesting.com
LVHW012008220924
791769LV00001BA/1